RISK
MANAGEMENT

DEDICATION
Sophie Ava Hopkin

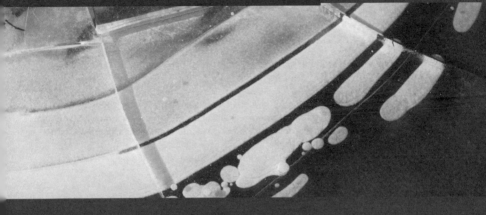

RISK MANAGEMENT

PAUL HOPKIN

KoganPage

First published in Great Britain and the United States in 2013 by Kogan Page Limited

120 Pentonville Road	1518 Walnut Street, Suite 1100	4737/23 Ansari Road
London N1 9JN	Philadelphia PA 19102	Daryaganj
United Kingdom	USA	New Delhi 110002
www.koganpage.com		India

© Paul Hopkin 2013

The right of Paul Hopkin to be identified as the author of this work has been asserted by him in accordance with the Copyright, Designs and Patents Act 1988.

ISBN   978 0 7494 6838 5
E-ISBN 978 0 7494 6839 2

British Library Cataloguing-in-Publication Data

A CIP record for this book is available from the British Library.

Library of Congress Cataloging-in-Publication Data

Hopkin, Paul.
  Risk management / Paul Hopkin. – 1st Edition.
    pages cm
  Includes index.
  ISBN 978-0-7494-6838-5 – ISBN 978-0-7494-6839-2 (ebk.)   1. Risk management.
I. Title.
  HD61.H5677 2013
  658.15'5–dc23
                                                                    2012051530

Typeset by Graphicraft Limited, Hong Kong
Printed and bound in India by Replika Press Pvt Ltd

CONTENTS

LIST OF FIGURES

PREFACE

Research released by the UK Cabinet Office a few years ago reported that the majority of small- to medium-sized businesses that suffered a major loss event, such as a fire or flood, became insolvent within 18 months of the disaster – even if they had full property insurance. A property insurance policy will pay compensation for most of the tangible costs – such as lost or damaged inventory, plant, property and equipment – however, much of the less tangible damage will not normally be covered by insurance. This can include damage done to the business' medium- and longer-term performance. While management is preoccupied with recovering from the loss event, existing customers may be lost, and opportunities for developing new products and/or securing new customers may be missed.

This all points to the importance of businesses paying attention to a full risk management programme. Risk management is about much more than just buying insurance for 'loss events', as Paul Hopkin shows in this book. It involves taking action to reduce the frequency and/or severity of possible loss events and having plans in place to respond after any event to mitigate the ultimate impact.

Paul Hopkin brings decades of experience in the application of the key principles and the practice of risk management. He has been a risk management consultant with a major insurance broker, a risk manager for several large companies, and is currently technical director at Airmic, the UK Risk Management organization. He has also been lead examiner on the International Certificate qualifications offered by the Institute of Risk Management for many years.

This book describes all the key steps in devising and implementing a formal risk management programme. It explains the various techniques available, together with providing checklists, templates and case studies. The five key steps are: (1) setting the risk agenda for the organization; (2) assessing the risks; (3) planning the responses to risks (controls to minimize risks pre-event, and plans for post-event disaster recovery and business continuity); (4) communicating risk policies and procedures; and (5) governance of risk with respect to all the various stakeholders in the organization.

All managers with operational responsibilities, not just risk managers, will find a great deal of useful material in this book. Other senior managers, even board members, will also find much to learn in the chapters covering risk communication and risk governance.

Alan Punter, January 2013

Dr Alan Punter was a risk management consultant with various international insurance brokers for over 25 years. He is now a Visiting Professor at Cass Business School, City University London and assistant chief examiner for the International Certificate and Diploma qualifications offered by the Institute of Risk Management. He also co-authored the research report Roads to Ruin, a study of major risk events commissioned by Airmic.

ACKNOWLEDGEMENTS

Risk management continues to be a very high profile management initiative. There are many risk professionals working in the different component parts of the risk management discipline and making a contribution to different types of organizations. This is, indeed, an exciting time to be a risk management professional.

I am grateful to the very large number of people who have helped (often unknowingly) with the development of the ideas that are included in this book. There is an international body of risk management professionals making a contribution to the development and successful application of risk management principles. This book draws on the conversations that I have enjoyed with many of these individuals. I acknowledge the rich source of risk management knowledge and expertise that is available on the websites of so many different kinds of organization. There is a fantastic resource of knowledge, experience and application that is available to all.

I have been the lead examiner for the Institute of Risk Management certificate course for the past six years. Many students have taken the certificate course during that time and I have met many of them on training courses. They have always been a source of knowledge and experience and I acknowledge their enthusiasm and the different approaches that they have discussed during the courses. I am pleased to acknowledge the contribution made to this book by discussions on ISO 31000 and COSO ERM.

Finally, I gratefully acknowledge the help and support of my wife, Joan, who has helped bring greater clarity to the text and helped overcome the worst mistakes associated with my weak spot of proofreading.

Figures 2.1, 7.2, 12.1 and 14.1 are included with kind permission of the Institute of Risk Management and are based on figures originally published in the 2012 Kogan Page book, *Fundamentals of Risk Management*, ISBN 978 0 7494 6539 1, **www.koganpage.com**.

Paul Hopkin

INTRODUCTION

> Risks are those events with the potential to have a significant negative impact on the organization. Risk management is a set of activities to ensure the best possible outcome after the event and/or achieve the most predictable consequences.

The nature of risk

Just like individuals, organizations have always faced risks. In fact, identifying the risks faced by an organization and then responding to them is not a new idea. However, the business environment for most organizations is becoming more risky; accordingly, organizations have to decide how to respond to this increased riskiness. Although the business environment has become more risky in recent times, there are many chief executive officers (CEOs) who are not yet convinced that a formalized approach to risk and risk management provides benefits that the well-established informal approach does not deliver.

To design a more formalized approach to risk management, a clear understanding of the nature of risk is required. A standard dictionary definition of risk is the chance that something unpleasant will happen. This gives rise to further questions associated with the chances (or likelihood) of the event occurring and the nature of the unpleasant outcomes (impact or consequences). Given that risks are generally considered to be unpleasant and/or unwelcome, this is a sensible starting point when planning a risk management initiative.

When an organization decides that it is going to set objectives and/or seek to deliver stakeholder expectations, there will be risks that can have a negative impact on the ability of the organization to achieve its aims. The achievement of objectives and/or the delivery of stakeholder expectations represent the rewards that the organization is seeking, but it inevitably faces risks that can have a negative impact on the fulfilment of those rewards. To keep the approach to risk simple and straightforward, risks can be viewed as events that could occur that would undermine the delivery of the desired rewards. For example, people participate out of choice in motor sports and other potentially dangerous leisure activities. In these circumstances, the return may not be financial, but can be measured in terms of pride, self-esteem or peer group respect. Undertaking activities involving risks of this type, where a positive return is expected, can be referred to as taking opportunity risks.

Sources of risk

Generally speaking, individuals do not deliberately seek risk. An individual may be seen as a risk taker, but the more accurate analysis is that the individual is seeking rewards that can only be achieved by taking risk. The same analysis will apply to organizations. An organization may establish a high risk strategy, and it is likely to be the increased rewards this strategy should deliver that will be the motivation for adopting such a strategy.

This is an important lesson for those who are seeking to persuade the CEO that a more formalized approach to risk management is beneficial. The formalized approach to risk management described in this book is based on the understanding that the CEO is seeking to deliver rewards to stakeholders. In presenting information about risks to such a CEO, it is important to provide information that aligns the risks with the delivery of those rewards.

All organizations have a vision or mission they are seeking to achieve, even if not set out in writing. The vision or mission will be delivered by instituting a strategy, devising tactics to deliver that strategy and designing appropriate operations. These will give rise to risks and managing the risks to strategy, tactics and operations will be the primary concern of the management of the organization. The other area of risk that is vitally important is the need to ensure compliance with all regulatory requirements.

To evaluate the anticipated consequences for strategy, tactics, operations and compliance, the organization will need to analyse risk events in terms of the potential impact on it. It is more straightforward to analyse risks in terms of the potential impact on finances, infrastructure, reputation and/or marketplace. This analysis can be undertaken with the help of risk management professionals and it then becomes the responsibility of top management to evaluate the anticipated consequences of these risks.

Risk management

Recent events in the world have brought risk into higher profile. Terrorism, severe weather conditions and the global financial crisis represent the extreme risks that are facing society and commerce, in addition to the daily, somewhat more mundane risks. Evaluating the range of risk responses available and deciding the most appropriate response in each case is at the heart of risk management.

Risk should be considered to be an event that will have a significant negative impact on an organization and/or result in significant deviation from expected outcomes. On that basis, risk management is about achieving the best possible outcome for the organization by preventing negative events, minimizing the damage done by those events when they do occur and containing the costs after the event. In other words, risk management is about achieving the best possible outcome in line with plans and expectations. By taking this approach, risk management activities will make the greatest contribution to the success of the organization and will become fully embedded in its strategy, tactics, operations and compliance activities.

Another important consideration for risk management is reducing the range of possible outcomes. For example, an organization may target a specific profit range for the trading period. The organization will want to manage events that could result in a lower than anticipated profit outcome, but it may also wish to maintain the profit within a certain range. Risk management tools and techniques such as hedging of interest and foreign exchange rates can be used to help manage this profit volatility.

Current status of risk management

The benefits of the successful management of risks have been understood for some time. There has been a transition during the past 20 years from the informal management of risks to a more formalized and process-driven approach. This changing nature of risk management has been motivated by the increased stakeholder expectation that organizations will identify the events that could significantly influence the performance of the organization and will also provide assurance that these events are being appropriately managed.

As well as the approach to risk management based on mandatory requirements and the need for assurance to stakeholders, there has been increasing awareness that risk management can bring significant benefits to the organization. The fact that risk management is a mandatory requirement for some organizations and/or seen as a competitive advantage by others has resulted in two different views of the contribution of risk management. These are referred to in this book as 'passive drivers' and 'proactive drivers' of risk management. The two approaches to risk management are described in more detail in Chapter 2.

Many organizations undertake risk management activities for passive reasons. This may be because risk management is a mandatory requirement, assurance is required for stakeholders and/or risk management information is required for decision-making processes. The proactive reasons for undertaking a risk management initiative are to improve the effectiveness and efficiency of strategy, tactics, operations and/or compliance. Both approaches to risk management are valid, but an organization needs to decide why it is undertaking risk management activities before embarking on a risk management initiative.

Successful risk management

There is no doubt that the business environment represents many and varied risks. This is true for all types of organizations, including commercial, charity and public sector, such as local authority, emergency services and central government. Therefore, organizations need to develop their own individual approach to the management of risk.

For most kinds of organizations, there is a mandatory requirement to undertake risk management. There is a danger that fulfilling this mandatory requirement will lead many organizations to introduce a very process-based approach to risk management. In many cases, this has resulted in a process that fulfils mandatory requirements but does not add to the success of the organization in a manner that can be clearly demonstrated or measured.

The intention of this book is to describe an approach to risk management that is simple and practical. Successful management of risk will contribute significantly to the overall success of an organization, but the actions taken need to be proportionate to the size, nature and complexity of the organization. Therefore, the manner in which this book is written is intended to ensure that the approach described is:

- simple and jargon-free by describing risk management as five easy steps;
- practical, through the inclusion of case studies, real-life examples and checklists;
- relevant by describing risk management as an integrated set of activities.

As the descriptions and discussions are simple and practical, the book does not provide a list of definitions nor include any abbreviations or acronyms that are not in common business use.

Implementing risk management

The managers of all organizations are aware of the level of risk embedded within the organization. However, few organizations actually evaluate the level of riskiness in a more formalized and structured manner. For risk management to achieve a useful purpose within an organization, evaluation of riskiness is a necessary starting point. Chapter 1 provides a simple checklist that will enable any organization to identify its level of riskiness.

Completing the riskiness index in Figure 1.1 will enable the organization to identify whether the risks it faces are primarily associated with finances, infrastructure, reputation and/or marketplace. From this simple indication of the level of risk within the organization, a more detailed analysis of the risks it faces and their potential impact can then be undertaken, normally with the assistance of risk management professionals. Having gained a view of the inherent riskiness within the organization, top management will then be able to evaluate the anticipated consequences arising from the level of risk.

The analysis of the potential impact of certain events is only a starting point. Top management needs to evaluate the anticipated consequences, so that further decisions can be taken, and will then be able to come to one of two conclusions regarding the potential impact and anticipated consequences of the risks identified: 1) the level of risk is tolerable and the information collected will be used to provide assurance to stakeholders and to support decision making; or 2) the level of risk is not tolerable and does not represent the most efficient and effective risk management standards for the organization.

Risk management cube

Figure I shows the risk management cube; it is a visual representation of the approach to risk management taken in this book. In simple terms, the risk management cube indicates that an organization should consider all of the potential impacts of risk on the finances, infrastructure, reputation and marketplace. The organization should then evaluate the anticipated consequences for strategy, tactics, operations and compliance.

To fulfil this approach, the organization should apply the five components shown on the front of the cube. These five components form the basis of the structure of the remainder of this book. They are easy to understand and do not separate risk management activities into those concerned with the risk management process and those concerned with the framework that supports the process.

FIGURE I Risk management cube

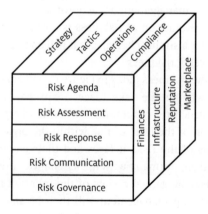

Risk management can, therefore, be seen as the five components of the risk management cube, each of which needs to be integrated into the existing activities and processes of the organization. The key benefit of this approach is that additional sources of management information and additional streams of management activities are unnecessary.

Risk management components

Having completed the riskiness index in Chapter 1, an organization will have a preliminary idea of its current status with respect to the significant risks embedded in its activities and processes. The organization will then be in a position to systematically review the five components of the risk management cube, as follows:

1 *Risk agenda* – this component requires the organization to set a clear understanding of why the organization undertakes risk management activities, as well as the main features of those activities.
2 *Risk assessment* – this component requires the organization to assess the potential impact on finances, infrastructure, reputation and marketplace and anticipate the consequences for strategy, tactics, operations and compliance.
3 *Risk response* – this component requires the organization to identify the existing and/or additional controls that are required, as well as the need for disaster recovery plans and business continuity plans.
4 *Risk communication* – this component requires the organization to establish roles, responsibilities and procedures, as well as to evaluate the requirements for a risk register and/or other form of risk action plan.
5 *Risk governance* – this component requires the organization to consider the expectations of stakeholders and provide risk assurance, as well as introduce governance procedures for existing and emerging risks.

Structure of the book

The book is presented in five parts to represent the five components on the front of the risk management cube. Part I is concerned with the risk agenda for the organization and includes a consideration of why the organization is launching a risk management initiative and the approach that should be taken to ensure that the initiative is proportionate, aligned and dynamic. The importance of ensuring that risk management is embedded in the organization is discussed, together with the need for appropriate monitoring of performance.

Part II considers the importance of risk assessment as a component of a risk management initiative. The need to analyse potential risks to finances, infrastructure, reputation and marketplace of the organization is considered. The responsibility of top management to respond to the anticipated consequences for strategy, tactics, operations and compliance is considered. Various risk assessment techniques are also considered, together with options for recording the outcomes of the risk assessment activities.

Undertaking a risk assessment will enable the organization to decide whether the current level of risk is tolerable. The decision on the tolerability of the risk will take account of the existing controls. The outcome of the risk assessment will be recorded in a risk register or risk governance report. The risk assessment will also identify situations where additional controls are required. If additional controls are required, the organization will need to implement additional risk responses and these will be set out in a risk action plan. This topic is discussed in Part III, together with descriptions of the various types of controls that are available: preventive, corrective, directive and detective. Part III also considers the importance of disaster recovery planning and business continuity planning, as well as the need to ensure the efficiency and effectiveness of the controls that have been selected.

Risk communication is vitally important and this has a number of features, as described in Part IV. For many organizations, the risk communication procedures are set out in a risk management policy. This risk management policy should consider the roles and responsibilities of individuals, as well as the terms of reference of committees with risk management responsibilities. The policy also needs to consider the various risk management procedures established in the organization, together with the relevant risk management performance and reporting requirements.

Many organizations undertake risk management because it is mandatory and/or because assurance is required that risk management procedures are in place. Part V considers the importance of risk governance and its relevance to the fulfilment of stakeholder expectations. Risk governance arrangements need to be in place for all organizations, whether the approach to risk management is passive or proactive. The management of emerging risks, together with the risks associated with managing stakeholder expectations, are also discussed.

Checklists and case studies

Throughout the book, the intention is to ensure a practical and realistic approach to risk management. Simple bullet point lists, short examples and practical hints are included within the text in each part of the book. At the end of each part, an extract from the report and accounts of a public limited company is included to illustrate the relevance of the topics covered. A short checklist of actions is also included at the end of each part, together with a list of further reading. To consolidate the lessons in the book into a fully worked example, Appendix 1 evaluates risk management within a fictitious weekly 'veggie box' delivery company called Organate Foods. Appendix 2 contains a number of templates for implementing a risk management initiative.

In summary, successful risk management can be delivered in five easy to understand steps:

1 Decide what risk management actions you are going to take and how you are going to take them by defining the risk agenda.
2 Analyse the potential impact and anticipated consequences of the risks faced by your organization by undertaking appropriate risk assessments.
3 Implement appropriate controls so that risks are managed to a tolerable level and the organization achieves the necessary level of resilience.
4 Develop and communicate the risk architecture and protocols for your organization and design a dynamic risk register and/or risk action plan.
5 Provide appropriate risk assurance to key stakeholders and ensure adequate governance of existing and emerging risks.

PART I
Risk agenda

> This component requires the organization to set the agenda for risk management, including a clear understanding of why the organization undertakes risk management activities and the main features of those activities.

Importance of the risk agenda

Part I is concerned with the risk agenda for the organization. The risk agenda component defines what the organization is going to do in relation to risk management and how is it going to do it. This will require identification of the passive and proactive risk management drivers for the organization, as well as the design of the features of the risk management initiative. Establishing the risk agenda starts with a consideration of why the organization undertakes risk management activities. This may be for passive reasons, such as:

- it is a mandatory requirement placed on the organization by regulators, customers or other stakeholders;
- there is a need to provide assurance regarding the existence of adequate risk management procedures; and/or
- risk management information needs to be available to make better informed business decisions.

Risk management activities may also be undertaken for proactive reasons and it is in these circumstances that the organization gains maximum benefit from risk management. The proactive reasons include the need to have efficient and effective:

- strategy and strategic decisions;
- tactics, including project identification and implementation;
- operations that are free from unplanned disruption;
- compliance with all relevant rules and regulations.

The risk agenda also includes consideration of the principles that will be followed or the features that will be incorporated when the risk management initiative is designed and implemented. Following these principles and incorporating these features will ensure that the risk management initiative itself is also efficient and effective. The principles that should be applied to the design and implementation of a risk management initiative are that risk management activity should be:

- proportionate to the level of risk faced by the organization, but comprehensive by considering all types of risks;
- aligned with all the activities and processes of the organization and embedded within those activities and processes; and
- dynamic and responsive to emerging risks, changing circumstances and developing situations.

The importance of the risk agenda is that it establishes the context within which risk management activities will take place. This will ensure that risk management activities are coordinated, but are always appropriate for the size, nature and complexity of the organization. These principles should be embedded within the risk management architecture and protocols for the organization.

Decisions about the scope of risk management activities within the organization and the reasons for undertaking those activities will ensure that they are always relevant and focused, while at the same time being suitable and sufficient for the organization. Establishing an appropriate risk agenda will maximize the opportunities for gaining benefit from those risk management activities.

Scope of the risk agenda

The scope of the risk agenda can be demonstrated by use of the risk management bow-tie. This simple diagram, shown in Figure PI, extracts information from the risk management cube shown in Figure I in the Introduction. It incorporates the key messages relevant to an effective risk agenda.

FIGURE PI   Risk agenda bow-tie

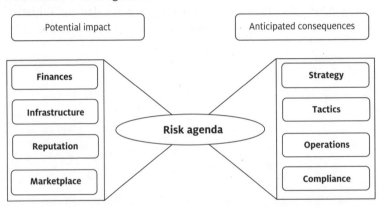

The risk agenda bow-tie illustrates that development of an appropriate risk agenda depends on consideration of the potential impact of risk events on the finances, infrastructure, reputation and marketplace of the organization. The risk agenda should also ensure that the organization makes appropriate plans to successfully manage the anticipated consequences of these events for strategy, tactics, operations and compliance.

Key messages for Part I

Part I is concerned with the organization's risk agenda, including consideration of why the organization is launching a risk management initiative and the features of the approach that should be taken. In summary, the key requirements are that risk management activities within an organization should be undertaken for explicitly identified reasons, either passive or proactive, as this will enable the organization to quantify the benefits that are being sought and ensure that they are achieved; and planned in a way that is appropriate for the size, nature and complexity of the organization and, in particular, the initiative should have features that are proportionate, aligned and dynamic.

CHAPTER ONE

RELEVANCE OF THE RISK AGENDA

Definitions and types of risk

The *Oxford English Dictionary* definition of risk is: 'a chance or possibility of danger, loss, injury or other adverse consequences' and the definition of at risk is 'exposed to danger'. In this context, risk is used to signify negative consequences. To undertake risk management within an organization, a definition of risk that is more aligned with business activities is required.

Risk in an organizational context is usually defined as anything that can impact the fulfilment of corporate objectives. This is a useful definition that is used by many organizations to define the risks to their activities and processes. However, it is helpful to clarify two issues: 1) whether risk can be attached to features of the organization other than corporate objectives; and 2) whether risk should always be considered as a negative.

The difficulty in attaching risks to corporate objectives is that the objectives may not be stated in full and they will often be established as annual objectives, usually associated with achieving change in the organization. However, it is possible to identify the risks faced by the organization by undertaking an analysis of its other features, such as the key dependencies, stakeholder expectations and/or core processes. These options for the attachment of risk are explored in more detail throughout this book.

In common usage, risks are considered to be events with an adverse outcome. This is an appropriate basis on which to plan risk management activities and is the approach that is taken in this book. In simple terms, risks may be considered to be those events with the potential to have a significant (negative) impact on the organization. The following box provides an example of the definition of risk used by an organization. It is worth emphasizing defining risk is a critical starting point for an organization and a vital component of the risk agenda.

Definition of risk used by a council:

Risk can be defined as the chances of something happening or not happening that will have an influence upon the achievement of business objectives. A risk can also be the failure to take advantage of opportunities to optimize the council achieving its planned objectives.

Considering risk to be associated with events that can only have negative outcomes is a useful and valid starting point for any risk management initiative. This will help bring clarity to the purpose of the initiative and will also have the benefit that the word 'risk' will be used in a way that aligns with everyday usage and understanding. Throughout this book, risk is used to indicate negative events and/or those events with an unacceptable level of uncertainty. This approach recognizes that the management of an organization is concerned with the rewards that the organization is seeking to achieve for stakeholders.

Compiling a risk description

Having decided on the definition of risk that will be used in an organization, the next step is to decide the information that will be required to adequately describe each risk. A detailed description is necessary to fully understand a risk. This will ensure that a common understanding of the risk can be shared across the whole organization and shared with stakeholders, as necessary.

There are many ways in which a risk can be defined and/or described. The purpose of establishing a list of features that will be collected about a risk is to ensure that the potential impact and anticipated consequences of the risk are understood. It is important that sufficient information is collected about each risk, but it is also important that unnecessary or theoretical information is avoided. This is consistent with seeking to ensure that risk management activities do not give rise to data that is unrelated to the information used to manage the organization.

The list below is consistent with the overall methodology for risk management described in this book. The focus is on keeping risk management activities relevant to the success of the organization. This means that information about risks should not be compiled in a way that is separate from managing the organization. Figure PI illustrated that risk management is not only concerned with an understanding of the potential impact of risks on the organization, but (more importantly) the anticipated consequences should the risk event occur.

The level of detail required when describing a risk will depend on the size, nature and complexity of the organization. However, to keep risk management as relevant as possible to the success of the organization, the following information about each risk is likely to be required:

- nature of the risk, including a brief description of the risk event and how it might be triggered;
- potential impact of the event on finances, infrastructure, reputation and/or marketplace activities;
- anticipated consequences for strategy, tactics, operations and/or compliance should the event occur;
- tolerability of the event in terms of likelihood of the event occurring and expected magnitude;
- existing control mechanisms, standard of control required and details of any related incidents and/or losses;
- plans for reducing the level of risk and details of responsibility and timetable for implementing the recommended improvements;
- details of how the level of risk is monitored and arrangements for communicating details of the risk to relevant stakeholders;
- confirmation of the governance arrangements related to the risk and any statutory or mandatory reporting obligations.

The amount of information that an organization collects about each individual risk would depend on the size, nature and complexity of that organization, and why the organization is undertaking risk management activities. It is important that an organization only collects sufficient information about each risk in order to fulfil the risk agenda. A key feature of the risk information collected should be that it relates to the overall success of the organization and does not represent a separate stream of management information.

Having collected the required risk information, the organization will then need to decide how that information will be stored and/or recorded. Risk management information software may be appropriate in some cases, but this will not generally be required. A simple record of the risk information may be adequate if the requirement is to provide assurance to stakeholders that risk management receives appropriate attention within the organization.

In some cases, the range of risks faced by the organization will be substantial and complex. There may be interdependencies between the risks and the analysis of potential impact and anticipated consequences may be technically difficult. In these cases, the organization may choose to present the information in a graphical form and/or keep the information in a software database. Risk management activities should always be proportionate for the level of risk faced by the organization.

Scope of risk management activities

In simple terms, risk management can be considered to be a collection of activities designed to produce the most desirable outcome should a risk event occur. These activities will include actions taken to: 1) prevent the risk event occurring; 2) minimize the damage should such an event occur; and 3) contain the cost of recovering from the event. The activities will also include actions that are taken to make the outcome of any risk event predictable and within a range that is tolerable to the organization.

Every organization that is undertaking a risk management initiative will need to decide the scope of that initiative. In deciding the scope, the risk agenda will need to be defined, by identifying why the organization is undertaking a risk management initiative and what it is attempting to achieve.

Chapter 2 discusses the drivers for undertaking a risk management initiative and identifies them as passive and proactive. Passive reasons for undertaking a risk management initiative relate to circumstances where the organization is seeking to collect risk information but is not intending to influence risk performance. The main concern, in these circumstances, would be to identify the level of risk in terms of the potential impact to finances, infrastructure, reputation and the marketplace. When the approach to risk management is proactive, the organization will be seeking to improve risk performance and thereby enhance the effectiveness and efficiency of strategy, tactics, operations and compliance.

> Scope of risk management defined by a hospital:
>
> *The objective of the risk management strategy is to promote a consistent and integrated approach across all parts of the organization embracing clinical, organizational and financial risks. It aims to do this through a robust governance structure, sound processes and systems of working and an open and fair culture of accountability that is focused on patient and staff safety.*

Establishing the risk agenda

As with all risk management activities within an organization, the risk agenda should be proportionate to the size, nature and complexity of that organization. The risk agenda needs to identify why the organization is undertaking risk management activities, how those activities will be structured and what benefits are expected. In simple terms, the risk agenda will define what the organization intends to do in relation to risk management and how those activities will be undertaken.

Decisions regarding why risk management activities are undertaken and the nature of those activities are part of establishing an appropriate risk agenda. The definition of risk that is used in the organization, together with a range of information that is collected about each risk, will also be part of that risk agenda. As with all aspects of risk management, the risk agenda cannot be established in isolation from the other activities and processes within the organization.

The risk management agenda will be designed to support the strategy, tactics, operations and compliance of the organization. An important part of a successful risk agenda will be to differentiate between outputs from risk management activities and the influence that the outputs are intended to have on the success of the organization. The output from the risk assessment activity will be the identification of the potential impact of risks on finances, infrastructure, reputation and the marketplace.

However, the concern of the management of the organization will be using this risk management output to evaluate the anticipated consequences for strategy, tactics, operations and compliance. Top management will receive information on the potential impacts and evaluate the anticipated consequences. It is the nature of the anticipated consequences that will enable management to plan suitable responses that enhance business success.

To decide on an appropriate risk agenda, an organization needs to have a view of the level of riskiness embedded within the existing strategy, tactics, operations and compliance. The list in Figure 1.1 provides a means of identifying the level of riskiness embedded within the organization. Understanding the level of risk faced by the organization will enable it to produce a suitable risk agenda that will then lead to the design and implementation of an appropriate risk management initiative.

In some ways, this can be considered to be the inherent level of risk faced by the organization and it represents a starting point for management to plan risk management activities. The riskiness index is structured in terms of finances, infrastructure, reputation and the marketplace. Under each heading, there are four areas of challenge for the organization. By providing a response to each challenge, it will be possible to identify the areas of greatest risk exposure or potential impact for the organization, as well as calculate an overall riskiness index for the organization (maximum score 80).

Having identified the overall riskiness of the organization, the risk agenda can then be established. As well as clearly identifying the motive(s) for undertaking risk management in the organization, the design and features of the initiative are vitally important. Chapter 2 considers the reasons for undertaking risk management activities in more detail. Chapter 3 identifies the features of the risk management initiative and describes how the initiative should be proportionate, aligned and dynamic. The box below is an example of a short statement whereby the organization defines its risk agenda.

FIGURE 1.1 Riskiness index

Award scores as follows:
1 = no problem; 2 = minor problem; 3 = major problem;
4 = serious problem; 5 = ruinous problem

Area of challenge	Score
1. Finances	
Lack of availability (or unacceptable cost) of adequate investment funds	
Inadequate procedures for allocation of funds to available opportunities	
Poor internal financial controls to prevent fraud and control credit risks	
Insufficient reserves for existing and historical liabilities (including pensions)	
2. Infrastructure	
Availability or cost of people skills, competencies and experience	
Inadequate premises, plant and equipment to support operations	
Processes, including IT infrastructure, have insufficient resilience	
Product availability inadequate, including supplier unreliability	
3. Reputation	
Poor public perception of the industry and/or organization brands	
Insufficient attention to ethics and corporate social responsibility	
High regulator involvement and compliance expectations	
Concerns over product quality and/or after sales service	
4. Marketplace	
Insufficient revenue generation or inadequate return on investment	
Competitive marketplace and/or rapidly changing product technology	
Poor sovereign economic health and/or lack of economic or political stability	
Complex supply chain and/or unpredictable raw materials costs	

Example of a risk management agenda

1   The aim of this document is to detail the corporate risk management agenda. It should be read by all managers who should explain it to their staff.

2   'Risk' is an event or cause leading to uncertainty in the outcome of the operations. For example, service standards are based on expected numbers of complaints. If more complaints are received, service delivery will fall unless staff are moved from other tasks to help. Conversely, if complaint numbers fall there is an opportunity to improve customer service.

3   We manage risk on a daily basis without describing this as 'risk management'. We consider what might go wrong and take steps to reduce the consequences if things do go wrong. However, we cannot rely on informal processes. Also, we must provide assurance to the stakeholders that we are managing risk correctly. We do need to formally identify corporate risks and mitigating actions.

4   The main responsibility for identifying corporate risks lies with managers. They should consider both existing risks and think about any new risks. Manager input is important as they are well placed to identify and monitor corporate risks.

5   The executive committee also has a role and, because of this, the risk register will be brought to relevant groups. Staff have a role in identifying corporate risks. The corporate risk register is available to staff and they are encouraged to contribute.

6   Risk needs to be considered when decisions are made. In particular, as corporate aims develop during the planning round, managers need to consider existing corporate risks; look at what we want to do over the next few years; and identify risks which may arise.

7   Projects and departments may have their own risk registers. Where a project risk is considered high priority it should be included in the corporate risk register. The project manager or steering group should advise management of any such risks. Managers may also identify risks to the aims of their department and mitigating actions should be included in business plans if considered serious enough.

CHAPTER TWO

DRIVERS OF RISK MANAGEMENT

Risk management drivers

Organizations undertake risk management activities for a variety of reasons. In many cases, these reasons are not explicitly stated. To ensure that the risk management initiative is proportionate for the organization, it is useful to explicitly identify why risk management activities are being undertaken. This will also help to ensure that the success of the risk management activities can be measured.

Drivers for undertaking risk management activities can be divided into two broad areas. Some organizations undertake risk management activities for passive reasons. These are based on monitoring risk management activities and using the information collected for assurance or decision-making reasons. Organizations that undertake risk management on a proactive basis will be seeking to influence the level of risk faced by the organization, and thereby further enhance the success of the organization.

Undertaking risk management activities for passive reasons is, of course, entirely legitimate. These activities will deliver benefits for the organization, in that it will gain a clear view of the level of risk that it faces and be able to explain the risks to other interested parties. In more detail, the passive reasons for undertaking risk management activities are:

- mandatory obligations placed on the organization by stakeholders, especially regulators, whereby risk management activities are designed to ensure fulfilment of governance rules and regulations;

- assurance is required by stakeholders, including the board and audit committee, that risk management and internal control activities are undertaken to an appropriate level;
- decision making is enhanced when appropriate risk-based information is available to support it, and risk management activities are focused on collecting that information.

Although undertaking risk management activities for passive reasons is often appropriate, greater benefits can be achieved if the requirement is to reduce the level of risk faced by the organization. The overall aim will be to improve the effectiveness and efficiency of activities and processes within the organization. Proactive risk management can make a substantial contribution to the success of the organization by enhancing the design and implementation of strategy, tactics, operations and compliance activities:

- Many organizations are now realizing the importance of risk management in the design and implementation of strategy. Embedding risk management activities within the development and execution of strategy will increase the chances of developing an effective strategy that is successfully implemented. In many ways, this is the ultimate challenge for organizations. However, to be generally accepted as best practice, there is a need to demonstrate that formalized risk management input into strategy design and implementation will provide additional benefits that may not reliably be achieved by a more informal approach.
- The contribution of risk management to successful implementation of tactics is becoming increasingly important. Tactics involve change initiatives and these are normally implemented by means of projects. Again, project risk management is a well-established and often fully embedded discipline that is making a significant contribution to the delivery of projects on time, within budget and to the required quality or specification.
- Risk management can make a considerable contribution to the efficiency of operations by achieving less disruption to normal processes. This contribution is often referred to as 'loss control' and is discussed in more detail in Chapter 12.

- Finally, the contribution of risk management to compliance activities is well established in areas such as health and safety and quality management. For some organizations, risk management activities are substantially focused on compliance requirements. In the finance sector, the Basel II requirements for banks and the Solvency II requirements for European insurance companies are compliance obligations that require significant risk management expertise to fulfil.

Passive drivers of risk management

The passive drivers of risk management relate to circumstances where it is mandatory, seeking to deliver assurance or is based on the collection of risk information. As a starting point, completion of the riskiness index provides an organization with an overview of the level of risk exposure it faces. The level of risk is often considered to be a combination of the likelihood of a risk materializing and the impact of the risk should it occur. While this is a useful analysis, the more important issue for organizations is the anticipated consequences for strategy, tactics, operations and compliance when the risk actually materializes.

To evaluate the consequences should a risk materialize, an organization should analyse each significant risk it faces in terms of likelihood and potential impact. This should be viewed as a necessary stage in evaluating the anticipated consequences, rather than the end of the risk assessment process. Analysing the level of risk can best be achieved by using the finances, infrastructure, reputation and marketplace risk classification system. The riskiness index referred to in Chapter 1 can be used as a preliminary means of evaluating the level of risk faced by the organization.

Awareness of the level of risk exposure using this structure will enable the organization to demonstrate the benefits it has obtained from a risk management initiative. The organization should evaluate the anticipated consequences of risk at the current level and confirm that the consequences are tolerable. If this is the case, the organization can confidently continue with the passive approach to risk management. Nevertheless, the organization would be well advised to evaluate the potential benefits that could result from reducing the level of risk exposure.

Passive drivers of risk management

The passive approach to risk management is illustrated by the risk management and assurance strategy for the provider of ambulance services. The organization acknowledges the importance of robust and transparent risk management and describes the mechanisms by which risk management is delivered.

It then describes the purpose of the assurance framework, which is to provide a structured process enabling the board to highlight any risks that may jeopardize the achievement of the strategic objectives and to provide assurance that controls are effectively operating to reduce the risks to acceptable levels.

The box illustrates that, although the organization allocates resources to risk management, the drivers of risk management are passive. The strategy described does not include reduction in risk exposure as a driver for undertaking risk management activities. Indeed, most organizations undertake risk management for passive reasons. Availability of risk information is valuable whether it is for mandatory reasons, to provide assurance or to facilitate decision making. Organizations that only undertake risk management for passive reasons will define their risk agenda accordingly and may well be entirely satisfied with the contribution that risk management is making.

However, many organizations recognize that risk management can make a greater contribution to the efficiency and effectiveness of activities and processes. Having evaluated the anticipated consequences of risks for strategy, tactics, operations and compliance, an organization may decide to improve risk performance. This can be described as a proactive approach to risk management and will deliver enhanced benefits and greater success for the organization.

Proactive drivers of risk management

It is no longer acceptable for organizations to find themselves in a position whereby unexpected events cause financial loss, disruption to normal operations, damage to reputation and loss of market presence.

Stakeholders now expect that organizations will take full account of the risks that may result in failure to implement strategy, late delivery of projects, unplanned disruption of operations and/or failure to ensure compliance.

The initial output from risk management is the analysis of the potential impact of identified risks and this is often referred to as the 'level of risk' or 'risk exposure'. If a proactive approach is adopted, the second output from risk management is the reduction of potential impact, which will provide benefits, as follows:

- *Finances* – will result in reduced cost of capital and better control of investment approvals.
- *Infrastructure* – will result in increased efficiency and competitive advantage, as well as improved supplier and staff morale.
- *Reputation* – will result in increased regulator satisfaction and an enhanced reputation and good publicity.
- *Marketplace* – will result in commercial opportunities being maximized and increased customer spend and satisfaction.

The overall benefits of proactive risk management can be summarized in a number of ways. By undertaking a risk management initiative for proactive reasons, more efficient and effective strategy, tactics, operations and compliance will be achieved. In practical terms, this will result in better strategic decisions, successful delivery of the correct projects, less disruption to operations and enhanced compliance. These are in addition to the benefits of passive risk management.

Achieving success in the reduction of the level of risk is only part of the contribution that can be made by risk management, albeit an important contribution. It is for the management of the organization to ensure that the reduced level of risk results in a more favourable set of anticipated consequences, should the risk occur. Also, the management should review the anticipated consequences and take advantage of any opportunities that may arise from the lower level of risk within the organization.

Business development model

There is no doubt that risks to organizations continue to increase, but a proactive approach to risk management will deliver enhanced efficiency and effectiveness of strategy, tactics, operations and compliance.

Part of the response to the increased riskiness of the business or commercial environment will be for the organization to continuously review and improve its business model.

Figure 2.1 provides an illustration of the business development model. In simple terms, it shows that the organization has developed a strategy for the future. This strategy needs to be evaluated in relation to the existing operations of the organization, so that tactics can be developed that will take the organization from its existing position to a position where it can deliver the strategy. Tactics represent the means by which strategy will be implemented and tactics, therefore, involve change.

Throughout this book, the word 'tactics' is used to cover the wide range of changes that an organization will need to make in order to

FIGURE 2.1 Business development model

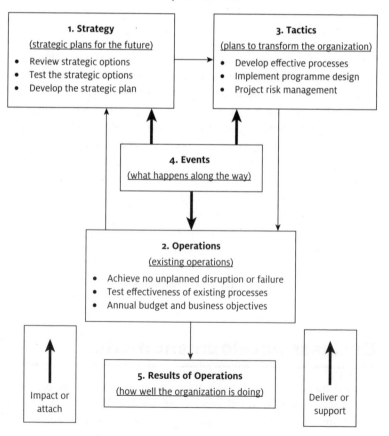

implement strategy. These changes will include product development, alterations to premises, plant and equipment, development of new workforce skills and changes to processes. Tactics could also include expanding into new work territories. Change is normally achieved through projects and a collection of projects is often referred to as a 'programme of work'.

The risks associated with projects can be considered as two broad types. The first is that the project may not be delivered on time, within budget or to the required quality or specification. These risks are managed by effective project management that includes a full consideration of risk management. However, the more important set of risks is that the improvement or enhancement anticipated may not be delivered by the project. For example, the decision to relocate certain business activities to a part of the world with lower labour costs may not achieve the desired outcome of reduced overall operating costs. This could arise for a variety of reasons, including lack of skill and expertise within the new workforce, more difficult communications within the organization and/or customer dissatisfaction with the new arrangements. Therefore, management will need to consider that, even if lower labour costs are delivered, other risks may increase. Otherwise, the overall result could be that labour costs have reduced, as anticipated, but the overall level of trade and/or profits for the organization has fallen.

Figure 2.1 illustrates that events occur that can impact strategy, tactics and operations. These events may be considered to be the risks associated with the business development plan. It is important that the risk management input into the business development model focuses on the significant risks that can have the greatest consequences for strategy, tactics, operations and compliance. Risk management will assist with the achievement of the best possible outcome with a reduced level of uncertainty or volatility about the outcomes.

Also included in Figure 2.1 is the notion that, at all times, the business development model has to communicate the results of operations. These results of operations must satisfy stakeholder expectations, including the need to ensure compliance at all stages in the business development model. This figure is also supportive of the fact that all organizations should seek to achieve a continuous improvement in performance; proactive risk management can make an important contribution to achieving this.

Figure 2.1 is also useful in identifying the concept of core processes. All organizations will have 'core processes' that represent the overall manner in which strategy, tactics, operations and compliance within the organization are designed and implemented. It is also worth noting that efficient and effective core processes are the means by which organizations deliver stakeholder expectations.

The example in the box below considers the range of consequences when an important player for a professional football club is injured. The football club is likely to have 'achieving success on the pitch' as a core operational process. Clearly, when a key player is injured, it will impact the ability of the football club to deliver that core process. Proactive risk management activities will ensure that the club has evaluated the potential consequences for this core process when a key player is injured. This example also shows that the identification, analysis and evaluation of significant risks can be undertaken using core processes as the starting point.

Range of consequences when a player gets injured

The players are a critically important asset for a professional football club. However, from time to time, key players get injured and the football club will need to consider the impact(s) of such an event well before it occurs.

If the injury is serious, a key player may be absent for a significant length of time. There are going to be substantial consequences caused by the long-term absence of the key player. These consequences will be most obvious on the pitch and the success of the team in matches is likely to be reduced. However, other consequences may also result and these could include the loss of revenue from the reduced sale of shirts and other merchandise linked to that player.

CHAPTER THREE

FEATURES OF RISK MANAGEMENT

Risk management principles

Chapter 1 considered the relevance of the risk agenda and the scope of risk management activities. It also discussed the importance of gaining a summary of the overall riskiness of the organization by completing the riskiness index. Chapter 2 considered the drivers for risk management in terms of what a risk management initiative should deliver. Although it is important to decide what the risk management initiative is seeking to achieve, it is also important to determine the features of that risk management initiative: that is what is considered in this chapter.

A risk management initiative should be defined by a set of principles. These principles apply to all types of organizations, regardless of the scope of the risk management initiative being introduced. To be successful, the risk management initiative should be proportionate, aligned and dynamic:

- *Proportionate* – risk management activities must be proportionate to the nature, size and complexity of the organization, but should also be comprehensive and consider all types of risks.
- *Aligned* – risk management activities need to be aligned with the other management activities in the organization and be fully embedded within all activities and processes.
- *Dynamic* – risk management activities must be dynamic and responsive to changing circumstances, so that the organization can successfully manage emerging as well as existing risks.

These principles represent the criteria that will be used when designing the architecture and protocols for implementation of a risk management initiative. They will also need to be reflected in the risk agenda that the organization establishes for itself. Clearly, the application of these principles will be specific to the organization and vary according to its size, nature and complexity. Although these principles are complementary, perhaps the most important principle when planning the risk management initiative is that it should be proportionate to the level of risk faced by the organization.

An organization will need to decide what it is seeking to achieve when launching a risk management initiative and the means by which those requirements will be delivered. In following the three principles set out above, the organization will devise a risk agenda that will pay due regard to internal and external factors relevant to the organization, the sector in which it operates, the range of activities that it fulfils and its overall culture.

Proportionate risk management

The organization will need to decide the resources that will be allocated to risk management. The resources that are required to implement the risk management initiative will be indicated by the architecture and protocols that the organization introduces. The architecture and protocols should embrace the principles of proportionate, aligned and dynamic. Perhaps the most obvious principle is that the architecture and protocols for implementing the initiative should be proportionate. Factors that will influence the extent of the architecture and protocols will include the level of risks faced by the organization and the regulatory framework for the business sector.

For example, in the finance sector there are strict regulatory regimes enforced by sophisticated regulators. Basel II requirements apply to the regulation of banks and the Solvency II requirements apply to the regulation of the insurance industry in Europe. Organizing risk management activities in a financial institution will require quite different levels of resource and expertise to those required in a non-regulated sector.

It is worth noting that, for financial institutions, risk management activities undertaken in response to Basel II or Solvency II will be compliance driven, so risk management activities will be substantially driven by passive reasons, but will, nevertheless, be very challenging and require significant resources. The box below describes the role of a chief risk officer in a financial institution; it should be noted that the job description does not include activities to reduce the level of risk faced by the organization. Nevertheless, the chief risk officer will be very senior within the organization and is likely to have a substantial department of qualified staff.

Role of chief risk officer

The chief risk officer position reports to the chief executive officer and facilitates the execution of risk management processes and infrastructure as a key enabler to achieving the business objectives of the organization with oversight of credit, market and operational risk and compliance. In summary, the primary responsibilities of the chief risk officer are as follows:

- Advise the board and senior management and support them in the establishment and communication of the risk management programme for the bank.
- Assist the CEO and executive team with developing and communicating risk management policies, risk appetite and risk limits.
- Facilitate risk assessments and monitor priority risks across the organization and help establish, maintain and continuously improve risk management capabilities.
- Promote a risk-aware culture of risk management and conduct risk management education and training.
- Implement appropriate systems, controls and risk reporting so that risk can be managed effectively and in a cost-effective manner.
- As a key member of the senior management team, help develop strategy in a manner which integrates risk management and controls.
- Advise senior management on the financial implications of risks related to key issues and important strategic decisions.
- Establish, communicate and facilitate the use of appropriate risk management methodologies, tools and techniques.
- Support the CEO and executive team with capital and resource allocation decisions.

The principle of being proportionate will apply to all organizations and will result in very different structures and resources for the risk management initiative. For a small organization such as Organate Foods, the case study in Appendix 1, the requirement for additional risk management expertise may be limited. The level of knowledge and experience of the management of Organate Foods will be adequate for most risk management tasks. When additional risk management expertise is required, this may be obtained on an outsourced or consultancy basis.

As well as decisions about the level of risk management expertise that needs to be available within the organization, decisions will need to be taken about the risk management architecture that is appropriate. Some organizations establish a separate risk management committee. For most organizations, this is disproportionate and discussions about risk management will take place at an existing committee, such as the board or the executive committee.

When setting up a separate risk committee, there are other considerations that will be taken according to what is proportionate. Decisions about the membership of the committee and the frequency of meetings will be determined by the role of the committee and the reporting line. For many organizations, the level of risk management resource that is proportionate is driven by regulatory requirements. Where an organization is not highly regulated, a separate risk committee with a high level of risk expertise and/or the appointment of a chief risk officer may be disproportionate.

Aligned risk management

Risk management activities need to be aligned with other activities within the organization, as well as embedded within the culture. An example of this alignment is related to the timing of risk assessment workshops. If the requirement on business units in the organization is that they produce the first version of the budget for the coming year in September, it is sensible for the annual risk assessment workshop to take place in August. This arrangement will ensure that the output from the risk assessment workshop is available for consideration as the budget is prepared.

If an organization has decided that committees of the board need to undertake a risk assessment of their activities at each meeting, it is logical for those meetings to take place with the same frequency as board meetings and about a month in advance. This will enable the committees to produce a report on recent activities and their risk management implications in time for each board meeting.

An important example of alignment of risk management activities is the requirement that a risk assessment should be included with each capital expenditure request. This will ensure that risk management and business investment decisions are aligned and that decisions are taken based on the best available information. Likewise, when a board discussion is scheduled on strategic options, consideration of the risks embedded within each strategic option should be evaluated at the same time as the strategic decision is taken.

The box below provides an example of how an organization can respond to changing technology and take advantage of the associated emerging risks. Such changes in technology will affect all organizations working in the same sector and successful organizations that respond to these emerging risks will gain competitive advantage. Other organizations that fail to respond will be at a disadvantage and may ultimately cease to exist. Changing technology is an example of what are sometimes referred to as 'emerging risks' and these are considered in more detail in Chapter 19.

Responding to changes in technology

A printing company operates in a very competitive marketplace that is undergoing important technological changes. In these circumstances, there are significant risks associated with the business and very important strategic decisions have to be taken. The company recognizes that the printing technology it currently uses is out of date and has to be replaced.

A risk assessment of strategic options has been undertaken, including an analysis of stakeholder expectations, existing customer requirements, existing staff skills, as well as a strengths, weaknesses, opportunities and threats, or SWOT analysis. The strategic options available to the company include outsourcing the printing work, sub-contracting and investing in new technologies.

Given the very substantial investment that would be involved, the company has decided that it will establish a joint venture with another printing company that operates in a non-competing sector. The new joint venture will jointly fund the investment in the new technology and thereby share the risk.

Embedding risk management within the organization is associated with the overall culture of the organization. Chapter 4 discusses the features that would be present in an organization that has successfully embedded risk management. These features can be summarized as leadership, involvement, learning, accountability and communication in relation to risk management.

Also, risk management frameworks have been developed that evaluate the level to which risk management activities are aligned and embedded. Compiling a set of structured questions will facilitate an evaluation of individual departments, locations or business units in terms of how well risk management activities are embedded within the facility. An appropriate set of challenges to determine the risk culture of a facility may include consideration of whether the organization has:

- a clear view of its purpose, including established objectives, policies and plans that have been successfully communicated;
- a commitment to shared values and policies that include accountability and trust to encourage the sharing of information;
- capabilities and skills and expertise, together with communication processes and appropriate control activities;
- a monitoring and learning environment that allows assumptions to be challenged and decisions made on whether information needs to be reassessed.

Dynamic risk management

All organizations have to be dynamic and responsive to change. It is, therefore, an important feature of the risk management agenda that arrangements are in place to ensure that the organization responds to changing circumstances. There are two stages to ensuring that the approach to risk management is dynamic. First, the organization should ensure that the risk register does not become a static document, but is more akin to a risk action plan. Second, the organization needs to establish specific monitoring arrangements that will give early warning that risk exposures are moving outside the range that the organization considers to be acceptable or tolerable.

For many organizations, the main risk management document is the risk register. There is a danger that this becomes a static record of the risks identified during a risk assessment workshop and does not provide any structure or motivation for improving the management of risk. This may be the case, even if the risk register contains information on additional actions that are required to improve the management of specific risks. This list may have no impact on the way in which risks are managed and may not even be reviewed again until the next workshop.

Unless an organization decides that it will take a dynamic approach to risk management, the production of a risk register can result in false assurance being given to stakeholders. (The important role that can be played by a risk register is discussed in more detail in Chapter 15.) For a risk register to be effective it needs to record appropriate information about each of the risks identified and describe the further actions that will need to be taken to reduce the level of risk. The most important danger to be overcome is that risk management is reduced to making lists of risks, even if the approach to risk management is passive.

Many organizations monitor indicators that provide information on relevant developments, both inside and outside the organization. These indicators may be lagging indicators, such as the extent of losses that have been caused by the particular risk, or they may be leading indicators. Leading indicators provide early warning that circumstances are changing in a way that may be detrimental. For example, international organizations will monitor exchange rate movements as these could have significant consequences for the organization. An organization with considerable debt will monitor interest rate movements as a leading indicator that the level of risk has changed.

The example below describes an expansion opportunity that has been identified by a football club. The risk agenda for the football club should identify how risk management will be considered as part of the evaluation of the opportunity. This is an illustration of an organization undertaking risk management activities for proactive reasons and ensuring that the approach is dynamic to emerging risks and changing circumstances. In this example, the group owns a football club as well as leisure and travel companies. It has identified developments in the marketplace that could give rise to further opportunities.

Expansion opportunity for a football club

The company has decided to look at opportunities for selling more products to the existing football supporter customer base. The company is currently formulating plans to investigate the viability of setting up a travel agency for fans of the football club who travel overseas, together with the provision of associated travel insurance. It is also considering the possibility of creating a football club credit card that will be managed by a new finance subsidiary.

The company will now need to look at the risks associated with these opportunities and devise a suitable programme of projects to implement the selected strategies. Ensuring that adequate account is taken of risk during all of these activities will increase the chances of selecting the correct strategy, designing the effective implementation tactics and, ultimately, ensuring efficient activities. At all stages in this design and development work, full compliance with statutory requirements is essential and can be included in the business development plans.

CHAPTER FOUR

PLANNING THE RISK AGENDA

Comprehensive risk agenda

The risk management agenda for the organization requires that two questions are answered: why is the organization undertaking risk management, and what are the appropriate architecture and protocols, bearing in mind the size, nature and complexity of the organization? The case study set out in Appendix 1 explores these questions for Organate Foods and the risk agenda for this 'veggie box' company. The reasons for undertaking risk management activities can be passive or they can be proactive, as discussed in Chapter 2.

The risk agenda developed by the organization needs to be comprehensive. However, that does not mean that it requires substantial resources or bureaucratic procedures. If the risk profile of the organization is simple and straightforward, additional risk management expertise beyond the knowledge and experience of existing managers may not be required. Likewise, in a small organization, it is possible that risk procedures, although they exist, will not need to be established in writing. In other words, the risk agenda has to be proportionate, as well as comprehensive.

Even in an organization where the risk management architecture and protocols are simple and straightforward, the organization should still ensure that a comprehensive risk management agenda has been, albeit informally, developed. The risk management agenda should pay regard to corporate objectives, stakeholder expectations, key dependencies for success and the core processes. Additionally, regard needs to be paid to the culture of the organization, available resources and legal and statutory requirements.

For many organizations, the risk management agenda will be established in writing. The case studies presented at the end of Part I provide an insight into the risk agendas for Oxfam, Leicestershire County Council and ITV (see pp 48–51). It can be seen that ITV has defined its risk agenda in terms of two main categories of risk. First, there are the high impact, low likelihood risks that would have a significant impact on the organization, but are unlikely to occur. As they are unlikely to occur, there may be no previous history to help develop the appropriate response. Also, it may be difficult to identify indicators that give early warning that the level of risk has increased or the anticipated consequences have changed.

Second, there are strategic risks that would impact the successful execution of strategy. The strategic risks are evaluated in relation to the strategic objectives established by ITV and the anticipated consequences should the risks materialize are considered. Also, ITV identifies process level risks, although these are said to be embedded into everyday activities within the organization. By clearly identifying the categories of risks that will be considered, ITV has established one of the key components of the risk agenda for the organization. The box below is another example of how an organization defines its risk agenda.

Defining the risk agenda

The risk agenda for an organization may be driven by mandatory requirements. This will define the resources that are required and may result in the organization defining the approach to risk management as follows:

- Risk management sits at the heart of good governance and needs to be embedded throughout all levels of the organization.
- Executive committee will determine whether the organization is 'risk taking' or 'risk averse', as a whole, or any relevant individual issue, and ensure risks are considered as part of every executive report decision.
- Executive committee will also ensure that procedures are in place to monitor the management of all risks with the appropriate controls in place.
- Awareness of risk management will improve corporate governance and the emphasis is on being risk aware rather than risk averse.

The risk agenda document on pages 49–50 identifies the risk management drivers for Leicestershire County Council. The document describes the benefits that will be achieved from the risk management initiative, together with the aims of the risk management strategy. In discussing the elements of the strategy, the document provides an insight into why Leicestershire County Council undertakes risk management activities and how they will be organized. The architecture and protocols described in the document give an insight into what Leicestershire County Council considers to be a proportionate response.

Embedded risk management

Risk management activities have to be embedded in an organization for them to be effective and achieve the desired benefits. Embedding risk management is one of the components of designing and implementing the risk management architecture and protocols that are appropriate for the organization, in terms of its size, nature and complexity.

Successful embedding of risk management, together with successfully aligning risk management activities and ensuring accountability for risk are related to achieving a satisfactory risk-aware culture in the organization. The level of risk maturity and the sophistication of risk management activities are also associated with the risk-aware culture. Various tools have been developed for measuring risk management culture within an organization, including software packages.

A list of components of a good risk management culture was discussed in Chapter 3. This formalized approach may be appropriate for some large organizations, especially where the audit committee has requested an objective evaluation of the risk culture in the different component parts of the organization. In circumstances where an in-depth analysis is not required and/or is disproportionate, an organization can still challenge its current level of risk maturity by considering what are generally recognized as the five components of embedded risk management, as follows:

1 leadership, whereby strong leadership exists with respect to embedding risk management into strategy, tactics, operations and compliance;

2 involvement of all stakeholders in the development of the risk agenda and the implementation of risk management activities;

3 learning risk management lessons with emphasis on training within the organization and learning from internal and external events;
4 accountability for risk and risk management but without an automatic blame culture when things go wrong;
5 communication, detailed reporting and openness on all risk management issues and the lessons that have been learnt.

Embedding risk management

A healthcare facility has decided to introduce a risk management initiative and ensure that it is embedded in the organization. The two important areas that have been considered relate to the benefits of embedded risk management and the key success factors in achieving this aim. The benefits of embedded risk management are widely recognized and include:

- reduction in management time spent 'fire-fighting';
- fewer sudden shocks and unwelcome surprises;
- more focus internally on doing the right things in the right way and therefore more likelihood of achieving business objectives;
- more likelihood of implementing change initiatives;
- strategy being appraised more effectively, leading to calculated risk taking; hence ...
- more confidence in moving into new areas; and
- overall cost of risk is reduced.

The key success factors in embedding risk management are related to the idea that the initiative is more likely to succeed if risk management is:

- supported by the board, publicly and privately, and communicated to everyone in the organization;
- sponsored by the senior management team and supported by experts in the specific risk areas;
- owned by business managers rather than departments such as insurance, risk management or internal audit;
- linked to clear strategic objectives at top level and to clear operational objectives throughout the organization;

- a priority for everyone because, no matter what their job, everyone has some responsibility for risk management and is measured as a personal objective;
- built on business processes already in place such as strategy reviews, planning, budgeting, insurance reviews, project appraisal and performance appraisal;
- expressed in a common language accessible to all members of the organization and given quality time by key management, including reports to the board.

Achieving measurable benefits

For a risk management initiative to be successful and sustainable, there have to be measurable benefits. If risk management is undertaken for passive reasons, the measurable benefits will be satisfying mandatory requirements, providing required assurance and having risk information available to support decision making. If risk management is undertaken because it is mandated by regulators, customers or other stakeholders, it should be relatively easy to demonstrate that good risk management activities take place in the organization.

For example, consider an organization has to file statutory report and accounts with regulators responsible for compliance with stock exchange requirements. Provided that the report gives an accurate description of suitable and sufficient risk management actions, regulators will be satisfied. It may also be that customers and financiers require reports on the risk management activities. The provision of adequate reports will satisfy these stakeholders that the actions they have mandated are actually being undertaken.

Certain stakeholders may require assurance that suitable and sufficient risk management activities are being undertaken and the significant risks are being managed to tolerable levels. Assurance may be required by external agencies, such as regulators and financiers, and they may also be required by internal committees or functions, such as the board, audit committee or the internal audit department. The box below describes the approach taken by an organization to achieve greater involvement of the board and ensure that the benefits of risk management are better understood.

Benefits of risk management

Together with other members of the risk committee, the board attended a risk management session. The session involved a short presentation on the benefits of risk management and how the discipline was being applied in the organization. Board members noted that, although the organization had been applying risk management principles for some time, one of the initial elements of the new risk management strategy would involve recording identified risks as a simple and proportionate response. This would be followed by a likelihood and impact analysis.

In this way, risk management would become embedded in the organization so that it was an inherent part of report writing and decision making. To gain a better understanding of risk management principles, board members undertook a group exercise to identify risks associated with the economic downturn. This highlighted the value of examining issues from all angles and that what at first seemed a negative environment might have some positive aspects that could benefit the organization.

When enhanced compliance is a driver for risk management, the benefits will be significant, but may not be measurable. Many regulators work on the basis that they will not provide positive assurance of compliance with statutory requirements. The regulator will point out, or even punish, non-compliance but would be reluctant to confirm that the actions taken represent full compliance.

Decision makers in the organization who require risk management data to make better informed decisions will be satisfied that risk management activities are bringing benefits if they are provided with adequate and accurate information. Providing such information for decision-making purposes is a vitally important activity, although somewhat passive. It is passive in the sense that the person requesting the information may not require that risk management standards are improved.

If risk management is being undertaken for proactive reasons, the challenge of demonstrating measurable benefits is more difficult, although successful risk management activities will be contributing to the overall success of the organization. In all cases of proactive risk management, the demonstration of benefits will be associated with:

- Achievement of business objectives and delivery of stakeholder expectations. In that way, risk management activities become embedded in the organization and the overall success of the organization relies on successful risk management.
- In these circumstances, the contribution of risk management will include support in the selection of appropriate strategy.
- Successful implementation of tactics will include enhanced business investment decisions and project delivery.
- Measurable results from risk management input into operations are easier to confirm. When an organization decides to introduce a loss control initiative, the reduction in the losses suffered by the organization is a clear demonstration of success. (Loss control initiatives are described in Chapter 8.)

Organizations taking a proactive approach to risk management will constantly seek information on changing and emerging risks. Sometimes, the organization will use internal lagging indicators. Indeed, these lagging indicators can be used to demonstrate the measurable benefit of risk management in terms of reduced disruption to operations and enhanced legal compliance, and will include reduced numbers of accidents at work for health and safety risks, and reduced data security breaches for data security risks.

PART I REVIEW

Checklist

This checklist for the risk agenda provides a list of four items that should be reviewed to confirm that an appropriate risk agenda has been developed for the organization. The starting point for developing an appropriate risk agenda is to complete a riskiness index (described in Chapter 1) and analyse the extent to which risk events could have a potential impact on finances, infrastructure, reputation or marketplace.

The overall objective of the checklist is to ensure that the organization has taken account of the issues considered in this part of the book. These issues include why the organization is undertaking risk management activities and considerations relevant to the risk management architecture and protocols that should be introduced.

The checklist is intended to focus on the priority risk management activities for an organization that is designing and implementing a comprehensive risk management initiative. It sets out the issues relevant to the risk agenda that need to be clarified by the organization.

1   Describe the passive reasons for undertaking the risk management initiative, including the extent to which risk management activities are undertaken because it is mandatory; to provide assurance to various stakeholders; and/or to collect information for better informed business decisions.

2   Describe the proactive reasons for undertaking the risk management initiative, including the need to improve the efficiency and effectiveness of activities associated with the design and implementation of strategy, tactics, operations and compliance.

3   Allocate resources to the risk management initiative that are proportionate to the level of risk faced by the organization, but sufficient to achieve comprehensive assessment, response, communication and governance of the significant risks faced by the organization.

4   Design risk management assessment, response, communication and governance activities so that they are aligned with other business processes, embedded within those processes and dynamic to changes that will affect the level of risk faced by the organization.

Case studies

Oxfam: risk management

The council of trustees has overall responsibility for Oxfam's system of internal control. Such a system of control can provide only reasonable, and not absolute, assurance against inappropriate or ineffective use of resources, or against the risk of errors or fraud. These risks are further heightened given the difficult nature of communications and institutional and financial infrastructure in some parts of the world where Oxfam operates.

There is clear delegation of authority from council through the chief executive to the rest of the organization. On an annual basis the major strategic and operational risks that Oxfam faces and the ways in which these are being monitored, managed and mitigated are considered by council. The control framework approved by council is subject to the following review and testing:

- Internal audit department carries out an approved programme of audits across all operations and activities, based on an agreed cycle of audits of the international programme and the major risk areas as identified by the council.
- Head of internal audit submits regular reports on audits conducted, risks identified and management's response to their findings, as well as an independent annual opinion on internal control.
- Control assurance report provides trustees with an annual opinion on the control environment.
- Both the external auditors and the head of internal audit meet annually with the trustees in private session independent of management.
- Trustees provide an annual report to council on its view of the control environment within Oxfam.

In addition, Oxfam has clear and easily accessible whistleblowing procedures in place and has a loss prevention team whose role is to investigate incidents of loss, theft or fraud, recover losses wherever possible and provide training for staff on incident management and reporting. These initiatives help ensure that breaches and weaknesses within the control framework are identified and investigated.

Council recognizes that, to achieve the objectives of the charity, the nature of some of Oxfam's work requires acceptance of some risks outside Oxfam's control – that is, risk that cannot be eliminated or fully managed – but where this happens there is active and clear monitoring of the risk. Council considers that systems and controls are in place to monitor, manage, and mitigate exposure to major risks. These include, among other control mechanisms, maintaining Oxfam's general reserves and the review of key systems and processes by the internal audit function.

(Based on information on the Oxfam website 2012.)

Leicestershire County Council: risk management policy

Leicestershire County Council believes that managing current and future risk is increasingly vital to the business of local government. It is therefore the policy of the council to adopt a proactive approach to the management of all risks that impact on its strategies, operations and the achievement of its objectives.

A certain amount of risk is necessary and unavoidable, but can be a positive force in the development of services. However, risks need to be managed and maintaining a robust system of risk management will enable the council to:

- Safeguard our clients, service users, employees, members, pupils and all other persons to whom the council has a duty of care.
- Preserve and enhance the services we deliver and support the quality of the environment.
- Protect our property, including buildings, equipment, vehicles and all other assets and resources and minimize our vulnerability to fraud and corruption.
- Maintain effective and efficient control of public funds and ensure and improve statutory compliance.
- Uphold and promote its reputation as a community leader, service provider and employer and deliver value for money.
- Secure trust from our stakeholders and partners through transparent and open management.

Aim of risk management strategy

The code of corporate governance for the council sets out a requirement to ensure that an effective risk management system is in place. The council has a statement on its approach to risk management and this strategy is intended to provide a basis on which that approach will be put into effect. The risk management strategy aims to:

- Establish clear roles, responsibilities and reporting lines for identifying and managing risks.
- Ensure that an appropriate level of risk management is consistently applied across the council.
- Increase awareness and reinforce the importance of effective risk management through shared learning of best practice and experience.
- Develop a culture across the county council where risk management is an integral part of key management processes.

Elements of the strategy

Leadership and responsibility – given the diversity of council services and the wide range of potential risks, it is essential that responsibility for identifying and taking action to address potential risks is clear.

Role of the corporate risk management group – given the wide variety of risks that face the council, and the differing circumstances that apply in different services, it is essential that there is consistency in the way that risks are identified and assessed. The establishment of a corporate risk management group has provided this consistency of approach. The group acts as a link between service managers, specialized groups dealing with particular areas of risk, senior management and members.

(Edited extract from the risk management policy 2010–2011, Leicestershire County Council.)

ITV: principal risks and uncertainties

In 2011 ITV continued to develop and review its risk management process. Our approach covers risks at all levels of the organization and examines business risks on both a top down and bottom up basis. The approach covers:

- high impact, low likelihood (HILL) risks – of low inherent likelihood but where there would be major consequences were the risk to materialize;

- strategic risks – would impact the successful execution of the strategy; and
- process level risks – embedded into everyday activity within the organization.

The board has overall responsibility for the content and operation of the risk management framework and performs regular review of both HILL and strategic risks. Process level risks are subject to ongoing review by internal audit. The board continues to review the appropriate risk appetite for certain risk types to ensure ITV is carrying an acceptable level of risk.

High impact, low likelihood (HILL) risks include:

1 *External economic and political environment:* major decline in advertising revenues, significantly impacting ITV's overall financial performance; ITV loses its credit status; collapse in investment values, leading to a material pension scheme deficit.
2 *Regulatory change or breach:* major regulatory breach that results in the loss of the Channel 3 licence, or the Channel 3 licence is not renewed in 2014.
3 *Critical failure in delivery model:* sustained denial of transmission facilities or the loss of a major data centre.
4 *Significant physical incident:* major incident results in ITV being unable to continue with scheduled broadcasting for a sustained period; major health and safety incident that results in a significant loss of human life.
5 *Prolonged cyber attack:* sustained cyber/viral attack causing prolonged system denial or major reputational damage.

Each strategic risk has been mapped to one of the four key strategic priorities and, where possible, assigned key risk indicators. Where appropriate, the key risk indicators are aligned to our key performance indicators and all of the strategic risks identified have been mapped to the four strategic priorities:

- create a lean, creatively dynamic and fit-for-purpose organization;
- maximize audience and revenue share from our existing free-to-air broadcast business;
- drive new revenue streams by exploiting our content across multiple platforms, free and pay;
- build a strong international content business.

(Edited extract from ITV, Report and Accounts 2011.)

Further reading

BSI (2011) *British Standard BS 31100 (2011): Risk Management. Code of practice and guidance for the implementation of BS ISO 31000*, www.standardsuk.com

COSO (2004) *Enterprise Risk Management – Integrated framework, executive summary*, www.coso.org

Financial Reporting Council (2005) *Internal Control. Revised guidance for directors on the Combined Code*, www.frc.org.uk.

HM Treasury (2004) *Orange Book, Management of risk – principles and concepts*, www.hm-treasury.gov.uk

Hopkin, P (2012) *Fundamentals of Risk Management*, ISBN 978-0-7494-6539-1, Kogan Page: www.koganpage.com

Institute of Chartered Accountants in England and Wales (2002) *Risk Management for SMEs*, www.icaew.com

Institute of Risk Management (2002) *A Risk Management Standard*, www.theirm.org

Institute of Risk Management (2010) *Structured Approach to Enterprise Risk Management and the Requirements of ISO 31000*, www.theirm.org

PART II
Risk
assessment

This component requires the organization to assess the events with the potential to impact finances, infrastructure, reputation and/or marketplace and then anticipate the consequences for strategy, tactics, operations and compliance.

Importance of risk assessment

Part II is concerned with risk assessment activities within the organization. The risk assessment component defines how the organization is going to identify the potential impact of events on finances, infrastructure, reputation and marketplace and the anticipated consequences for strategy, tactics, operations and compliance. Implementing the risk assessment component starts with a consideration of how organizations should identify and assess the significant risks that it faces.

Risk assessment involves the identification of events that could impact the organization. The potential impact of these events should be analysed; this is discussed in Chapter 6. Completion of the riskiness index will provide the organization with an overview of its risk profile and enable the organization to identify weaknesses and plan appropriate actions. The range of risks that need to be identified can be described as:

- *financial risks*, including inadequate funds, incorrect investment decisions, poor internal financial control and inadequate reserves;
- *infrastructure risks*, including risks associated with people, premises/plant and equipment, processes and product availability;
- *reputational risks*, including perception of the industry, corporate social responsibility, regulator activities and product quality;
- *marketplace risks*, including insufficient revenue generation, actions of competitors, health of the economy and supply chain risks.

Risk identification and analysis is often led by risk management professionals and this will result in identification and analysis of potential impacts. However, it is the responsibility of the management of an organization to determine the anticipated consequence of each of the identified events and design and implement appropriate responses in relation to:

- *strategy* and the significant risks to the overall long-term mission, aims and objectives of the organization;
- *tactics* and the effectiveness of processes, as well as the significant risks to implementation of strategy, including management of projects;
- *operations* and the significant risks to the efficiency of operations, including disruption associated with people, premises, processes and products;
- *compliance* with all applicable rules and regulations, especially in highly regulated sectors.

Decisions about the scope of risk assessment activities that will be undertaken within the organization and the procedures for undertaking them should all be considered. The primary requirement is that risk assessment activities are proportionate to the size, nature and complexity of the organization.

The scope of risk assessment should include attention to the aims and objectives of the organization. However, it is also important to consider the expectations of stakeholders, the key dependencies of the organization and the presumptions that underpin business planning. The importance of emerging risks should not be underestimated and the increasing complexity of supply chains should also be considered when undertaking risk assessments.

It should be remembered that the primary reason for undertaking risk assessments is to analyse the current level of risk faced by the organization and decide whether the existing controls are effective and efficient. Additionally, risk assessment activities have an important role to play in the ability of the organization to fulfil mandatory and statutory requirements, provide assurance to stakeholders and support decision making within the organization.

Scope of risk assessment

The scope of risk assessment activities can be demonstrated by use of the risk management bow-tie. This simple diagram, shown in Figure PII, extracts information from the risk management cube shown in Figure I in the Introduction. It incorporates the key messages relevant to effective risk assessment.

The risk assessment bow-tie illustrates that development of appropriate risk assessment activities depends on consideration of the potential impact of risk events on the finances, infrastructure, reputation and marketplace of the organization. Risk assessments should also ensure that the organization successfully evaluates the anticipated

FIGURE PII Risk assessment bow-tie

Key risk assessment actions:
- Assess impact of risk to finances, infrastructure, reputation and marketplace
- Assess consequences of risks for strategy, tactics, operations and compliance

consequences of these events for strategy, tactics, operations and compliance.

Key messages for Part II

Part II is concerned with the arrangements for undertaking risk assessments within the organization; these assessments should always be relevant and focused. When undertaking risk assessments, the organization should ensure that all significant risks are identified, analysed and evaluated. This will involve consideration of the potential impact of risks, as well as the anticipated consequences, as follows: the potential impact of risk needs to be analysed, bearing in mind that a risk can impact one or more features of the organization, such as the finances, infrastructure, reputation and marketplace; and risk will be associated with all of the business activities and processes within the organization and it is necessary to identify the anticipated consequences of risks for strategy, tactics, operations and compliance.

CHAPTER FIVE

RELEVANCE OF RISK ASSESSMENT

Aims of risk assessment

Risk assessment is the second component of the risk management cube shown in Figure I in the Introduction. Undertaking risk assessments that are suitable and sufficient is a vitally important activity that helps to deliver the risk agenda and underpins successful risk response, communication and governance. A risk assessment of any feature of an organization can be undertaken, including departments, locations, projects and budgets. However, the structure of the risk assessment activities in the organization needs to be decided.

The approach taken in this book is designed to evaluate the overall influence of risk management on the success of the organization. Therefore, the main components of the risk management cube relate to the analysis of those events with the potential to impact finances, infrastructure, reputation and marketplace. However, risk management activities have to be relevant to the success of the organization. Therefore, part of the assessment process is also concerned with evaluating the potential consequences of the event for strategy, tactics, operations and compliance.

The most obvious purpose of a risk assessment is to identify all of the risks that could impact the feature that is being assessed. An analysis is then undertaken of the level of risk associated with each of the events that has been identified. The final stage is the evaluation of the anticipated consequences of the risk. The output from the risk assessment exercise then enables the organization to decide whether the current level of risk and potential impact and/or anticipated consequences is acceptable or tolerable.

Undertaking risk assessments

The following is a statement that can be found in the annual report and accounts of many companies regarding risk assessments:

The board considers risk assessment, implementation of mitigating actions and internal control to be fundamental to achieving the group strategy. Internal control provides the board with reasonable but not absolute assurance. The board has an ongoing process for identifying, analysing, evaluating and managing significant risks faced by the group and maintains a risk register.

If the current level of risk is acceptable or tolerable, the primary purpose of the risk assessment is associated with assurance and governance of risk within the organization. However, if the current level of risk is not acceptable, further control measures need to be introduced. In this case, the primary purpose of the risk assessment is to ensure that necessary risk improvement recommendations are designed and implemented.

Although risk assessment is normally considered to be a means of validating the existing controls, the purpose can often be wider. In some circumstances, undertaking a risk assessment may be a control in its own right. For example, if a new procedure is introduced to reduce the level of risk, the new procedure will need to be assessed. If the result of that assessment is that the new procedure is satisfactory, undertaking the risk assessment has provided confirmation that the level of risk is now tolerable.

Another important purpose of risk assessment is to decide whether any of the existing controls are unnecessary and can be removed. For example, if a warehouse no longer stores high value bonded goods, the existing level of security arrangements may be inappropriate. The risk assessment provides an opportunity to evaluate these controls, remove unnecessary ones and thereby save money and make existing operations more efficient.

It is good practice to review risk assessments on a regular basis, depending on the level of risk. Also, if circumstances change, the risk assessment will need to be reviewed. The organization or another organization in the same sector may suffer losses in situations where it appears that the level of risk has changed. In these circumstances, it is appropriate to undertake a repeat risk assessment to further validate the existing controls. This is another example of the updated risk assessment acting as a control in its own right.

Risk assessment techniques

There are a range of risk assessment techniques; probably the most common is the use of brainstorming sessions, normally during a risk assessment workshop. If the risks being evaluated are physical risks, inspections and audits are also an effective means of undertaking risk assessments. In certain circumstances, checklists and questionnaires can be used as the basis of undertaking risk assessments. The key features of these techniques are:

- *Workshops and brainstorming* – collection and sharing of ideas at workshops to discuss the events that could impact the objectives, core processes or key dependencies. The advantages are that consolidated opinions can be gathered from all parties and the greater interaction at a workshop produces more ideas. The disadvantages are that senior management may tend to dominate the discussions, and important risks may be missed if relevant people fail to attend the workshop.
- *Inspections and audits* – physical inspections of premises and activities and audits of compliance with established systems and procedures. The advantages are that physical evidence is used as the basis of forming opinions and a good structure will be used when analysing information. The disadvantages are that inspections are only suitable for physical risks and the audit approach will tend to focus on historical experience.
- *Checklists and questionnaires* – checklists and questionnaires have the advantage that they are usually simple to complete and are less time-consuming than some other risk assessment techniques. However, this approach suffers from the disadvantage that any risk not referenced by appropriate questions may not be recognized as significant.

Risk workshops are probably the most common of the risk assessment techniques. Brainstorming during workshops enables opinions on the significant risks faced by the organization to be shared. A common view and understanding of each risk is achieved. The organization should be aware that members of staff undertaking specific tasks will often have the most accurate view of the risks involved. The views and experiences of all staff need to be represented and considered during the workshop discussions.

When organizing a risk assessment workshop, it is important to focus on the reasons for undertaking the assessment and the desired outcomes from the exercise. In summary, the most important outcomes from any successful risk assessment exercise will be:

- identification and analysis of all the significant risks and the evaluation of the consequences of each risk event;
- confirmation of whether the current level of control is adequate and/or the existing level of risk is tolerable;
- validation that additional controls need to be introduced, or (perhaps) some controls are unnecessary and can be removed.

Collecting information on risk exposures

One of the key decisions when planning risk assessment activities will be who to involve in the risk assessment exercise. Sometimes risk assessments are undertaken by the board of directors as a top-down exercise. Risk assessments can also be undertaken by involving individual members of staff and local departmental management. The importance of consulting staff who actually undertake the work should not be underestimated.

The opinion of the chief executive officer (CEO) is critically important, especially as it helps to define the overall attitude of the organization to risk. There is no doubt that the CEO will be able to provide a well-structured view of the significant risks faced by the organization; the disadvantage is that the focus is likely to be on external risks. Although the CEO will be aware of the financial and infrastructure risks, these internal risks and the day-to-day management of the organization may not be his or her major concern or area of interest.

In general, the overall approach by the organization to risk assessments will be heavily influenced by the risk assessment techniques that are selected. It is important that the approach selected is consistent with the culture of the organization. The participation of appropriate individuals is critical to the success of risk assessment activities: all relevant individuals should find the time to participate in the risk assessment activities.

In addition to the knowledge and information possessed by individuals, the risk assessment exercise will require other information and data. The information that is required when evaluating the anticipated consequences for strategy and/or tactics will be different from the information required when evaluating the consequences of risk events for operations and compliance.

Assessment of strategy and tactics will require information that is similar to that obtained during a due diligence investigation. If the strategy involves expansion of the organization into new territories and/or new products or services, the organization may not have the experience of the risks that could be involved. Likewise, implementation of that strategy by way of tactics or projects could require the organization to obtain information from outside the organization itself.

When undertaking a risk assessment of operations and/or compliance, more of the information is likely to be available from within the organization. In the case of risk assessment of operations, the risks to the infrastructure that supports those operations need to be identified, analysed and evaluated. For certain types of risk, loss information will be available from a variety of sources, such as:

- loss data from within the organization itself;
- reports of losses suffered by competitors;
- research reports evaluating business options;
- consultancy firms and professional advisers;
- trade association and networking meetings.

There will be circumstances where there is insufficient information available to undertake a full risk assessment. Nevertheless, top management of the organization may need to make a decision and implement plans. The absence of adequate information may be because of developing technology, changing consumer habits, developing litigation environment, unknown legal framework and/or new strategy for the organization. (These circumstances represent emerging risks, as considered in more detail in Chapter 19.)

Some risks may be considered to be emerging risks because the information is not available or has not yet been discovered. In this case, all organizations faced with that risk are in the same position and will need to make decisions based on incomplete information. In other circumstances, a risk that is considered to be an emerging risk for one organization may be fully understood by another organization. An example of the requirement for specific risk information when undertaking a risk assessment is described in the following box.

Sources of risk data

The following provides an example of the sources of risk information that may need to be used when undertaking a specialist risk assessment, such as the assessment of aviation risk:

There is no known source of information or analysis tools that directly and specifically supports assessing the scale (in terms suitable for contingency planning) and nature of aircraft incidents. The consequence of incidents can, generically, be considered qualitatively by reference to past incidents, with judgements about specific scenarios expressed quantitatively.

Tools have been developed to assess the magnitude of incidents in any one location, but these tools tend to require specialist expertise and software. Their results could be drawn on for the sake of contingency planning though, such as by defining the physical size of incidents and area affected, for example. Accordingly, aviation risk is amenable to quantitative risk assessment with a reasonable level of certainty.

As a further example, an international restaurant brand is seeking to expand its activities into a city where it has not previously traded; this will represent an emerging risk for that organization. Restaurants already trading in that city will have more information about customer behaviour and the associated risks will be well-known. The restaurant already trading in the city will have sufficient information to analyse and evaluate operating and compliance risks. The restaurant seeking to expand into that city will not have the same level of information from its own experience and may consider the risks involved to be emerging risks for the organization.

This example leads to the conclusion that emerging risks can be characterized as those risks for which the organization does not have sufficient information. The risks and uncertainties associated with these emerging risks are greater for the organization that does not have sufficient information. In this example, the existing restaurant should be aware of the fact that other restaurants in the city are relocating to a more fashionable district. Therefore, the newcomer has a higher risk of opening the new restaurant in the wrong part of the city.

SWOT and PESTLE evaluations

To help have a structured discussion at a risk assessment workshop, there are several brainstorming formats in common use. These may be qualitative or quantitative, depending on the level of analysis of the risk that is required. One of the most common of the qualitative brainstorming structures is the SWOT assessment of the strengths, weaknesses, opportunities and threats faced by the organization. SWOT analysis will lead to the identification of:

- *strengths* – internal or external to the organization and these may relate to a strong position in one or more of the finances, infrastructure, reputation and/or marketplace of the organization;
- *weaknesses* – also internal or external to the organization and may likewise relate to a weak position in one or more of the finances, infrastructure, reputation and/or marketplace of the organization;
- *opportunities* – can relate to better use of the internal resources, but are more often associated with external features that enable the organization to gain greater rewards from strategy and tactics;
- *threats* – can also relate to inefficient use of internal resources, but likewise are often associated with external features that would prevent the organization from gaining appropriate rewards from strategy and tactics.

The SWOT analysis has the benefit that it also considers the rewards available to the organization from the opportunities in the external environment. One of the strengths of the SWOT analysis is that it can be linked to strategic and tactical decisions; a danger is that it is not a structured risk classification system and, therefore, there is a possibility that not all of the significant risks will be identified.

The other common qualitative approach is the PESTLE analysis that considers the political, economic, social, technological, legal and ethical (or environmental) risks faced by the organization. PESTLE is a well-established structure with proven results for undertaking brainstorming sessions during risk assessment workshops. PESTLE is not a risk assessment technique, but rather a risk classification system that can be used when planning a workshop or designing lists and questionnaires.

The PESTLE structure can be used to undertake assessment of strategy, tactics, operations and/or compliance. However, PESTLE is most easily applied to operational and compliance risks. It can be used as an alternative to using the finance, infrastructure, reputation and marketplace structure when undertaking the initial identification and analysis of risk events.

CHAPTER SIX

ANALYSING POTENTIAL IMPACT

Assessing potential impact

A structure for risk identification is required to identify all of the risks facing an organization. Formalized risk classification systems enable the organization to identify where similar risks exist within the organization. Classification of risks also enables the organization to identify who should be responsible for setting strategy for management of related or similar risks. Also, appropriate classification of risks will enable the organization to better identify the risk appetite and total risk exposure in relation to each risk, group of similar risks or generic type of risk.

Benefits of risk assessment

Undertaking risk assessment is now an established part of managing an organization. The requirement to facilitate the completion of a risk assessment is sometimes suggested to the organization by regulators. For example, the following appears on the City of London Police website:

Officers from the City of London Police licensing department are able to support your event or promotion by risk assessing it. The purpose of this is to enable us to give you appropriate advice to ensure your event is safe. This process is entirely voluntary, except in cases where the City of London Corporation has made it a condition of your licence. To carry out this assessment, we require certain information about the event from you, as listed on our risk assessment form.

The identification of risks that have the potential to impact finances, infrastructure, reputation and marketplace represents a risk classification system that will be applicable to almost all types of organization. The contribution of risk management specialists is to assist with the identification of the potential impact of events on these categories of risk. It is then the function of the management of the organization to assess the anticipated consequences of these types of events on strategy, tactics, operations and compliance.

As with so many risk management decisions, it is for the organization to decide which risk classification system most fully satisfies its needs and requirements. The identification of a suitable system is fundamentally important and will facilitate improved management of risk. The PESTLE risk classification system is a widely used system and was discussed in Chapter 5.

In addition to establishing a suitable risk classification system, there is a need to align the timing of the risk assessment workshops with other activities within the organization. For example, if an organization does not normally hold meetings and workshops, then a workshop may not be the most appropriate approach to risk assessments. Likewise, if the culture of the organization relies heavily on reports and written papers, then this will be the best way of conducting the risk assessments.

In view of the importance of company reputation, it is worth considering the specific issue of reputation risk, especially if the organization operates in a very competitive marketplace. The inclusion of reputation risk as a separate category of risk is not universally accepted. It is sometimes argued that damage to reputation is a consequence of other risks materializing and should not be considered as a separate risk category. However, reputation is vitally important, particularly when organizations are seeking to use their brand name to enter additional markets, or achieve 'brand stretch'.

Risk magnitude and likelihood

Most organizations produce a series of definitions to enable the magnitude of the risk to be identified in a little more detail. A typical set of definitions of risk magnitude for a city or municipal authority would be as follows:

- *Major* – major loss of service, including several important areas of service and/or protracted period of severe disruption in excess of five days with major impact on achievement of several key targets and objectives.
- *Significant* – complete loss of an important service area for a short period or a significant effect on services in one or more areas for a period of weeks with significant impact on achievement of a key target or objective.
- *Moderate* – moderate effect on an important service area for a short period and/or adverse effect on services in one or more areas for a period of weeks with moderate impact on achievement of one or more targets or objectives.
- *Minor* – brief disruption of an important service area and/or minor effect on non-crucial service area resulting in disruption for less than one day with minor impact on achievement of targets.

Having identified the possible magnitude of the impact, the organization needs to define the range of possible likelihoods of the event occurring at or above the significant level. Again, using the example of a city or municipal authority, a typical set of definitions of likelihood would be as follows:

- *Very likely* – more than 75 per cent chance of occurrence of an event that is expected to occur in most circumstances and/or frequently encountered with an imminent chance of occurrence.
- *Likely* – 51 to 75 per cent chance of occurrence of an event that is expected to probably occur in many circumstances but not a persistent issue, although it has happened in the past or elsewhere.
- *Unlikely* – 10 to 50 per cent chance of occurrence of an event that is not expected to happen, although it has occurred at some time in the past, but is not likely in all the current circumstances.
- *Very unlikely* – less than 10 per cent chance of occurrence of an event that may occur only in exceptional circumstances and has not been known to happen in the recent past.

By assigning a measure of magnitude and a measure of likelihood to the risk, the level of risk can be determined. This will lead to the identification of the priority risks. Many organizations will find that the total number of risks identified in a workshop is between 100 and 200; after the risk analysis has been completed, it is typical that this is reduced to between 10 and 20.

Although most organizations combine likelihood and magnitude into a single measure called 'level of risk', this approach is not always helpful. For example, an industrial or warehouse business could assign the same 'level of risk' number to a high likelihood low impact event, such as forklift truck damage to buildings, as to a low likelihood and high impact event, such as a major fire. A report that indicates the same level of risk for both events does not give top management enough information to be able to determine the anticipated consequences of each event.

Quite different risk responses would be appropriate in these different circumstances. It is likely that driver training would be a suitable control to reduce the incidence of forklift truck damage to buildings, whereas insurance would be the appropriate control for the risk of a major fire. It is important, therefore, to recognize the limitations of assigning a single level of risk number to a risk, as the output from a risk analysis exercise. It may be more useful to assign a number to potential impact of each risk event and, separately, indicate the likelihood of the event giving rise to a significant impact.

Top management of the organization should take the information from the risk assessment workshop and develop appropriate plans. These plans will be based on the anticipated consequences should the risk occur. Top management will sometimes take the view that the risk is so unlikely to occur that pre-planning is unnecessary or a waste of resources. This approach is based on the decision by top management that only foreseeable major events will have disaster recovery and business continuity plans developed. If the event is very unlikely, top management may decide that the event will be managed as a crisis, with the necessary resources being made available in response to the exact circumstances.

Risk assessment considerations

It is necessary to decide the structure of the risk assessments and whether they will be undertaken by department, location or budget, and the categories of risk that will be evaluated (the importance of risk classification systems is discussed in Chapter 7). Having identified the subject of the risk assessment, the assessment itself can take place.

For the sake of example, consider the assessment of a business unit or subsidiary of the organization. Undertaking a risk assessment that is suitable and sufficient involves four basic steps:

1 Identify the events that could have an impact on the finances, infrastructure, reputation and/or marketplace of the organization.
2 Determine whether the magnitude of the potential impact could be above the defined significant level for the organization.
3 Complete the analysis of the risk by determining the likelihood that the potential impact will be above the defined significant level.
4 Analyse whether the potential impact and/or identified likelihood is tolerable for the organization.

A sensible approach to risk assessment is to look at the potential magnitude of the risk as the main criterion when evaluating the anticipated consequences and planning appropriate responses. In simple terms, the organization needs to identify the magnitude of a risk event that would be significant. So that an organization can concentrate on significant risks, a test for risk significance is required.

The list below provides suggestions on the type of benchmark tests that could be used to decide whether the impact is significant. For risks that will have an impact on finances and marketplace, the benchmark test is likely to be based on monetary value. For risks that could disrupt the infrastructure or routine operations of the organization, a benchmark test based on the impact, cost and/or duration of disruption is appropriate. For reputation risks, the most likely benchmark will be based on the adverse publicity that would result if the risk materializes. The list below is a typical indication of benchmark levels for an organization:

● significant risks to *finances* would have an impact on the balance sheet of more than 0.5 per cent turnover and/or an impact on the profit and loss account of more than 5 per cent annual profit;
● a significant risk to *infrastructure* would cause disruption to normal operations of more than half a day and/or an increased cost of operation exceeds 10 per cent budget;
● a significant risk to *reputation* would cause the share price to fall by more than 10 per cent and/or would result in the event being reported on national TV, radio or in newspapers;

- a significant risk to the *marketplace* would have an impact on the balance sheet of more than 0.5 per cent market capitalization and/or an impact on the profit and loss account of more than 5 per cent annual profit.

This benchmark test for significance is an important step in the development of a robust approach to risk assessment. Having clearly established the magnitude of risk that would be of concern to the organization, further analysis can then be undertaken as to how likely the event would be to cause that magnitude of impact or loss. It should be remembered that analysis of magnitude and likelihood are outputs from the risk assessment workshop. Management is responsible for evaluating the anticipated consequences and developing the appropriate response(s).

Risk appetite and risk criteria

An important part of the evaluation of anticipated consequences will be a consideration of the risk appetite of the organization. It is a very difficult concept to precisely define and apply in practice; it is sometimes considered to be defined by the risk criteria established by the organization. The risk appetite or risk criteria are an important component in the risk evaluation phase of the risk management process. It should be remembered that consideration of risk appetite cannot be taken in isolation from the anticipated rewards associated with strategy, tactics, operations and compliance for the organization.

One of the fundamental difficulties with the concept of risk appetite is that, generally speaking, organizations will have an appetite to continue a particular operation, embark on a project or embrace a strategy, rather than a direct appetite for the risk itself. In other words, risk appetite and risk exposure should be considered as a consequence of business decisions rather than a driver of those decisions. Consideration of risk appetite should normally take place within the context of other business decisions, rather than as a stand-alone decision.

When considering risk perception and risk appetite, it is worth reflecting on the fact that certain individuals may be more concerned about a low impact risk with a high probability of occurrence (such as a car crash) than they will about a high impact risk that is unlikely to happen (such as an earthquake). This difference in approach is often reflected in the risk assessment process and can affect the way in which significant risks are prioritized.

Many organizations face risks that are an unavoidable part of their core processes. For example, a news broadcaster will need to send reporters into dangerous or hostile environments if it is to present up-to-date news. Management will take all actions to reduce the risks to the news team so that the potential impact and anticipated consequences become tolerable. These actions may include training for the news team, detailed plans should an injury or unauthorized detention occur and/or instructions to the news team to withdraw from the area in certain defined circumstances.

At all times, the management of the organization will be evaluating the risks to the news team in terms of the anticipated rewards. The rewards in this case will be enhanced reporting of the news events. Steps can be taken by way of training and the introduction of procedures to ensure cooperation between news broadcasters to reduce the risks. However, it is unlikely that the news broadcaster will describe the risks to its reporters as acceptable or within a predetermined set of risk criteria. Nevertheless, the news broadcaster will have to get to the stage where the risks to news reporters are considered to be tolerable, or risks that the organization is willing to take. The nature of the BBC guidance related to work in hostile environments is considered in more detail in one of the case studies at the end of Part III (see pp 133–134).

Judgement will be required by risk managers when determining the potential impact of an event. The use of that information to determine the anticipated consequences is for top management in the organization. Management is responsible for planning the actions that will be taken according to these factors. It is also for management to decide what risks they are willing to take, including the high impact/low likelihood risks. Ultimately, the position has to be reached where all risks become tolerable for the organization in relation to the rewards that are anticipated.

CHAPTER SEVEN

EVALUATING ANTICIPATED CONSEQUENCES

Range of consequences to consider

There are many risk classification options open to organizations. Financial institutions, for example, will classify risk as market risk, credit risk and operational risk. Market risk relates to the risks associated with financial markets, such as changes in interest rates and foreign exchange rates. Credit risks are associated with lending money to a borrower that is unable to pay it back. Operational risks relate to the financial consequences of operational disruption and dysfunction.

Other types of organization will seek a wider risk classification that does not focus entirely on risks to finances. This book uses a risk classification system based on the potential impact to finances, infrastructure, reputation and/or marketplace. Organizations may use this approach, or an alternative risk classification system that focuses on the analysis of risks to key dependencies, stakeholder expectations and/or core processes. Identification of risks as strategic, tactical, operational and compliance is a system that classifies risk according to their business consequences for the core processes in the organization.

Having identified the risks facing the organization, there is a need to undertake a risk analysis that will identify the potential impact for finances, infrastructure, reputation and marketplace. For many organizations, the list of identified risks could be between 50 and 100, or in some circumstances, even more. Having identified this long list of risks, the next stage is to analyse the potential impact of these risk exposures, both in terms of likelihood and magnitude of the risk events occurring. As discussed in Chapter 6, this is one of the outputs of the risk assessment exercise.

This output is communicated to top management who undertake the evaluation of the anticipated consequences. This risk evaluation phase will be based on the risk exposure information or the potential impact information provided by risk management specialists. Top management will be concerned with the core processes in the organization and will need to evaluate the anticipated consequences of the various risks in terms of strategy, tactics, operations and compliance.

However, individual organizations will decide on the risk classification system that suits them best, depending on the size, nature and complexity of the organization and its activities. Many risk management standards and frameworks suggest a specific risk classification system. If the organization adopts one of these standards, it will tend to follow the classification system recommended, but there is a danger that the risk classification system used by risk professionals is not aligned with the way the management of the organization classifies risk. To bring maximum benefit to the organization, it is important that risk professionals align their terminology with that used in the organization.

The risk classification system that is selected should be fully relevant to the organization concerned. There is no universal classification system that fulfils the requirements of all organizations. In fact, it is likely that each risk will need to be classified in several ways to clearly understand its potential impact and anticipated consequences.

Scope of risk assessments

To make the risk assessment as relevant as possible to the management of the organization, the features that would be the subject of risk assessment are likely to be related to strategy, tactics, operations and compliance. Although risk assessment of operations and compliance is the best established approach, assessment of strategy and tactics also needs to be undertaken. The example in the following box, from the pharmaceutical industry, illustrates the wide scope of risk management and assessment activities in a complex organization.

Scope of risk management

Protection of patient by managing risk in the quality systems and manufacturing process is being given prime importance in the pharmaceutical industry. The scope of risk management extends to every product and every process associated with risks. It is important that product quality should be maintained throughout the product lifecycle.

A risk management programme starts with identifying the possible risks associated with a product or with the process used to develop, manufacture and distribute the product. An effective quality risk management ensures the high quality of drug product to the patient. In addition, quality risk management improves decision making if a quality problem arises. It should include systemic processes designated to coordinate, facilitate and improve decision making with respect to risk.

Undertaking assessment of strategy should be fairly straightforward. The organization will have its existing strategy and a risk assessment of this can be undertaken. Certain risks will be embedded within that strategy and, by implication, those risks are tolerable to the organization. These represent the risks that the organization is willing to take to achieve its strategic objectives.

In addition to the risk assessment of existing strategy, organizations need to undertake risk assessments of all alternative strategies it may be considering. This may be a time-consuming activity, but it will ensure that risk management activities achieve the greatest benefit for the organization. Most organizations will tend to settle on a strategy and then undertake a risk assessment of that strategy. This approach is satisfactory, provided that the strategy is amended to take account of the risk assessment and the assumptions that underpin the selected strategy are tested as part of the risk assessment.

Undertaking an assessment of tactics has two major components. Tactics are the means by which strategy is implemented and changes brought about in the organization. Some organizations have a project or capital expenditure approval system that is based on risk assessment. The approach taken is that all projects need to be justified on the basis that they reduce risk. This is a viable means of selecting tactics and identifying appropriate projects, on the basis that reducing risk should enhance rewards.

Assessing tactics should involve risk assessment of the range of projects that are available to the organization. Again, it is common for organizations to put forward capital expenditure proposals and then assess the risks embedded within that proposal. Ideally, organizations should assess all available projects and tactics but this may be overly burdensome. As well as assessing the risks involved in achieving the change intended by the project, the risk assessment should also include assessment of the risks that are embedded within delivery of the project itself.

The most familiar use of risk assessments is in assessing operations and compliance. Many types of risk assessments are undertaken, depending on the size, nature and complexity of the organization. For organizations involved in activities with significant health and safety risks, the completion of health and safety risk assessments is usually a statutory requirement. Organizations such as casinos and others that handle large amounts of cash will undertake specific fraud risk assessments.

Purpose of risk assessment

The purpose of all risk assessments is to validate the controls that are currently in place, decide whether additional controls are required and/or remove any unnecessary controls. If risk management is to make a positive contribution to the success of the organization, risk assessment of operations should also involve assessment of inefficiency and make recommendations to improve the cost-effectiveness of the operations.

Risk assessment of compliance is becoming increasingly common. The requirement placed on organizations listed on a US stock exchange is that they undertake a risk assessment of their financial reporting arrangements to ensure that the financial status of the organization is accurately reported. Risk assessment of the compliance challenges for financial institutions is another area where risk management can make an important contribution to the success of the organization.

Compliance issues are most important for highly regulated organizations. This is an increasingly large proportion of all organizations and includes companies listed on a stock exchange, local and central government departments, charities, financial institutions, betting and gaming organizations, as well as those involved in a wide range of healthcare activities. For many organizations involved in healthcare, risk management is at its most relevant when seeking to achieve compliance with the many relevant codes of practice.

The motivation can go beyond the need to comply with mandatory obligations. In some cases, satisfactory compliance is a requirement of the licence to operate. Poor compliance standards will result in withdrawal of the licence and the organization will either have to close down and/or the existing management will be replaced. This sanction exists in many countries in relation to hospitals and related health services, as well as schools. In some cases, there is the additional benefit in that a highly compliant organization may be able to apply for a status that gives its management greater flexibility. For example, the ambulance service described in the box below may be able to gain access to additional independent funding if it can demonstrate consistently high levels of compliance with the relevant codes of practice.

Risk management in the ambulance service

Healthcare services operating ambulances will have a range of obligations placed on them, such as speed of response, training of staff, availability of equipment and cleanliness/decontamination of the vehicle. There may be considerable benefits for the organization in achieving high levels of compliance with the standards that have been set down for these various issues.

Ensuring high levels of compliance will require accurate risk assessment of the events that could interfere with that high level of compliance. This is a valid application of risk management principles, but the motivation is primarily compliance, rather than the efficiency and effectiveness of strategy, tactics or operations.

Risks to core business processes

It is worth remembering that risk assessments are undertaken to analyse the potential impact of events and then evaluate the anticipated consequences for the organization. The output from the risk assessments will help the organization determine whether the level of risk is tolerable for the organization.

Figure 2.1 (page 28) described the business development model in terms of strategy, tactics and operations. The figure shows that when an organization decides on a strategy, it needs to take account of its existing operations. Tactics, by way of change projects, are then planned to transform the organization to a position where it can deliver the intended strategy.

In developing an overall business model, an organization will need to pay regard to the mission statement as the high level statement of what the organization is seeking to achieve. The organization will then need to produce strategic and/or business plans to deliver the mission statement. To validate the mission statement, strategy and business plans, the organization needs to pay regard to internal and external factors.

Figure 7.1 provides an analysis related to that in Figure 2.1 and considers strategic, tactical, operational and compliance core processes. In Figure 7.1 core processes are used to identify the high level processes that deliver stakeholder expectations. In simple terms, a core process is something that is designed to deliver a set of stakeholder expectations; a good example is a football club, where 'deliver success on the pitch' will be a core process. By focusing on core processes, management will ensure that a broad view of business activities is embedded in the organization. Attaching the risk management activities to core processes will align risk management activities with the drivers for the organization.

The internal assessment included in Figure 7.1 can be undertaken by means of the analysis of strengths, weaknesses, opportunities and threats (SWOT) described in Chapter 6. The internal assessment, together with the mission statement, will result in a set of corporate objectives for the organization. The external assessment can be carried out by a second SWOT analysis. The external assessment, together with the mission statement, will result in the identification of stakeholder expectations. (The concept of stakeholder expectations is discussed in more detail in Chapter 20.)

FIGURE 7.1 Core business processes

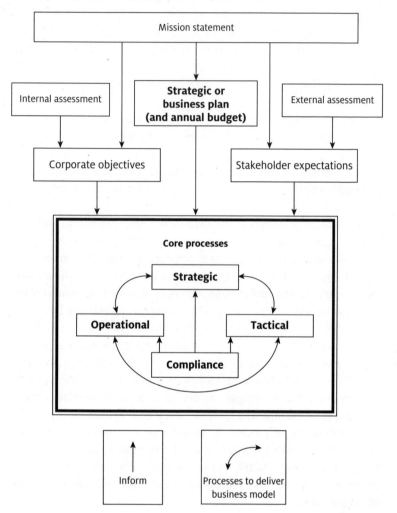

By concentrating on core processes, it is possible for risk management activities to be aligned with the management of the organization. Even if an organization does not use the terminology related to core processes, the essence of the approach is obvious. All organizations have collections of related activities that can be described as core processes. These collections of core processes will be designed to deliver strategy, tactics, operations and/or compliance.

In both Figures 2.1 and 7.1, compliance requirements underpin all of the activities of the organization. For some organizations, compliance is a major concern that requires specific and separately planned management activities. An example is the need for European organizations in the insurance sector to comply with the requirements of the European Directive on the solvency of insurance companies, known as Solvency II. Compliance with Solvency II requirements will demand robust compliance core processes supported by significant resources.

Linking stakeholders and success

IKEA is a very successful retail organization and the following comment is adapted from information on the IKEA website:

IKEA has modified the value chain approach by integrating the customer in the process and introducing a two-way value system between customers, suppliers and IKEA. In this global sourcing strategy, the customer is a supplier of time, labour, information, knowledge and transportation. On the other hand, the suppliers are customers, receiving technical assistance from IKEA through various business services.

The company wants customers to understand that their role is not to consume value, but rather to create it. IKEA seeks to mobilize suppliers and customers to help them further add value to the system.

The development of corporate objectives, together with a clear understanding of stakeholder expectations will assist with the development of the risk agenda; this is illustrated by the example of IKEA. The risk agenda needs to pay due regard to the following:

● *Risks to strategy* are usually long-term risks that impact the ability of the organization to maintain the core processes concerned with the development and delivery of strategy. The organization needs to confirm that the risks embedded in strategy are the risks it is willing to take and that they are justified by the potential rewards.

- *Risks to tactics* are usually medium-term risks that impact the ability of the organization to maintain effective core processes concerned with the management of tactics, projects and other change programmes. The organization needs to confirm that it has sufficient resources to implement the strategy by means of projects and programmes of work.

- *Risks to operations* are usually short-term risks that impact the ability of the organization to maintain efficient core processes concerned with the quality, continuity and monitoring of routine operations. The organization needs to confirm that the operations will run smoothly, compliantly and without inefficiency or unplanned disruption.

- *Risks to compliance* can be associated with the long-, medium- and short-term activities and processes that can impact the ability of the organization to maintain compliance within these activities and processes. The organization has to confirm that adequate compliance can be achieved and maintained in relation to strategy, tactics and operations.

CHAPTER EIGHT

UTILIZING RISK ASSESSMENTS

Recording the results of the risk assessment

When a risk assessment is undertaken, the results will need to be recorded. The way in which this is done will be related to why the assessment was undertaken. If the risk assessment was undertaken for mandatory, assurance or decision-making reasons, a risk register that forms the basis of a risk governance report will be the appropriate means. If the risk assessment is undertaken for decision-making reasons, it will be typical for the outcome of the risk assessment to be attached to the business proposals. For example, a risk assessment should be attached to a strategy proposal so that the risks embedded in the proposed strategy can be evaluated by decision makers. When tactics are being planned, risk assessment of the proposed tactics is an essential business planning procedure. The risks associated with following the proposed tactics need to be evaluated, as well as the risks embedded in the project(s) that will bring about the required change. These are the risks associated with project selection and project delivery, respectively.

Risk assessment of routine operations is also required. Therefore, risk assessment of both annual budget proposals and routine operations need to be undertaken. Likewise, risk assessment of the obstacles to achieving compliance, both in operations and in the business model, need to be recorded. In short, the organization needs to decide why it is undertaking risk management activities in order to be sure that the correct format for recording the output from the risk assessment exercises is established.

If the organization is undertaking risk management activities to improve efficiency and effectiveness of strategy, tactics, operations and compliance, the use of a risk register may not be the most appropriate means of recording the results of risk assessments – developing a risk action plan is a more dynamic means of using and recording the output. If the risk action plan becomes an integral part of, for example, project management, the contribution of risk management will be increased and guaranteed. In simple terms, there is a danger that producing a risk register serves only to produce a document that has a list of the significant risks faced by the organization, but fails to make a contribution to the business success of the organization.

The danger associated with the risk register simply being a list of risks is much reduced when an organization undertakes risk management activities for proactive reasons. In these circumstances, the risk register will develop into the risk action plan and will become an integral part of managing the organization. Therefore, the most effective records of a risk assessment exercise are records that have taken the output from the risk assessment exercise, converted it into a risk action plan which, in turn, becomes the basis for improving effectiveness and efficiency of the organization's strategy, tactics, operations and compliance.

Developing a risk action plan

For organizations that undertake risk management for passive reasons, a well-constructed risk register is a very useful and effective means of recording the current status of risk management activities within the organization. The risk register can form the basis of a risk governance report to the board, audit committee and other stakeholders requiring assurance on the status of risk and risk management.

The risk register will record the results of a risk assessment and provide useful insight into the risk status of the department, location, project or other feature that is being assessed. In many ways, undertaking a risk assessment is itself a control activity. When used in this way, the ultimate objective of the risk assessment is to decide whether the risks that are being taken are acceptable, comply with the established risk criteria and/or are within the risk appetite of the organization. In overall terms, the risk register will confirm that the current status of the risks faced by the organization is tolerable.

Therefore, the use of a risk register as a tool for passive risk management is invaluable. It can demonstrate that there is compliance within the organization with respect to risk management, it can provide assurance to relevant stakeholders and it can assist with decision making. However, there are limitations to the use of a risk register and there is a danger that it records a snapshot of the status of the organization with no incentive to improve the standards of risk management.

Developing a risk action plan

The questions set out below demonstrate that a school is taking a proactive approach to risk management and is seeking to achieve specific benefits from the risk management initiative.

Current situation

- Do we have a robust risk management policy and process in place and how and to whom do we need to communicate the policy and process?
- Do the risk management policy and process support our school improvement priorities?
- Are there opportunities for staff and governors to discuss and understand what risks are facing the school?
- Do we track the performance of our risk management strategies against agreed outcomes?

Improvements

- Are our 'significant risks' (critical impact risks) clearly identified and mitigation actions integrated into the current action plan?
- Are we confident that systems in place are effectively managing our medium and lower priority risks satisfactorily?

Achieve these

- What processes exist to embed risk management into the school culture and how do we monitor implementation and effectiveness of risk strategies?
- What is an appropriate review cycle and who will ensure that outcomes are appropriately reviewed?

- Is there potential to attend courses/events/receive information to improve our risk awareness and understanding?
- Do we get regular progress reports on risk management and any amendments made to the risk register for the school?
- Did our efforts make the difference we wanted to see (as set out in the school risk action plan) and what do we do next?
- Is there any independent evaluation of our progress available?

If the organization wishes to take a proactive approach to risk management, the status of the risk register needs to be upgraded to that of a risk action plan. The box illustrates a proactive risk management approach taken by a school. The proactive reasons for undertaking risk management are to improve the effectiveness and efficiency of strategy, tactics, operations and compliance. The emphasis on the need to improve performance means that the risk action plan should specify the improvements that are required to controls and seek to quantify the benefits that are expected to result.

It is standard practice for the risk register to include details of required improvements to controls and thereby reduce the potential impact of risk events. However, it is unusual for the risk register to identify the anticipated benefits that are required. By developing the risk register into a risk action plan, the organization can anticipate the benefits it is expecting to receive. The organization will be taking risks, but they must be appropriate for the level of reward that is achieved. It is the responsibility of top management to ensure that this risk to reward equation is correctly balanced.

Disruption to operations and loss control

All organizations face the possibility of events that can impact their operations. These can cause unplanned disruption and/or inefficiency. Loss control is a risk management initiative that identifies and seeks to control the potential impact of an event before it occurs, during the event and during the recovery phase. These three components of loss control are usually referred to as loss prevention, damage limitation and cost containment. Implementing a loss control initiative is an example of a proactive approach to risk management that is required to produce tangible and measurable benefits.

Typically, the sorts of events considered during a loss control initiative are insurable risks or perils and will include fire, storm, flood, theft and injury. The discipline of risk management has strong origins in the management and control of insurable risks. Normal efficient operations may be disrupted by loss, damage, breakdown, theft and other threats associated with a wide range of dependencies and these may include people, premises, processes and products. These are the same four categories used in the riskiness index referred to in the Introduction. It is worth evaluating these four components in more detail, in terms of the risks that can arise, as follows:

1 *People* risks are related to the availability of necessary people skills and expertise and include lack of people skills and/or resources, inappropriate behaviour by senior managers, unexpected absence of key personnel and ill-health, accident or injury to people.
2 *Premises* risks are related to the available ability of premises, plant and machinery and include inadequate, insufficient or inaccessible premises, damage or contamination of premises, and damage to and/or breakdown, theft or loss of physical assets.
3 *Processes* risks are related to unplanned disruption of processes and include failure of IT hardware or software systems, disruption by a hacker or computer virus, inadequate management of information and failure of communication or transport systems.
4 *Products* risks are related to products and services and include poor product or service quality, disruption caused by failure of suppliers, delivery of defective goods or components and failure of outsourced services and facilities related to the products or services.

The approach taken by a loss control initiative is to use the output from a risk assessment and convert it into a risk action plan that will reduce the anticipated consequences of events occurring and thereby make a significant and measurable contribution to the efficiency and effectiveness of operations within the organization. The loss control initiative will result in the risk register of potential impacts being converted into a risk action plan of measurable loss control programmes. It is worth briefly considering the three components of a loss control initiative in more detail:

1 *Loss prevention* is about reducing the likelihood of an adverse event occurring. Loss prevention will also be concerned with making plans and arrangements to reduce the magnitude of an event that does occur.
2 *Damage limitation* is concerned with reducing the magnitude of the event when it materializes. The contribution of damage limitation will be greatest if planned actions can be implemented as the event is actually taking place.
3 *Cost containment* is about reducing the impact and consequences of the event. It will ensure the lowest cost of repairs and include business continuity plans to ensure that the organization can continue after the loss event.

Damage limitation in relation to fire hazards is well established. Although sprinkler systems are often considered to be a loss prevention measure, they are, in fact, the major control for ensuring that only limited damage occurs when a fire breaks out. Other damage limitation factors related to fire include the use of fire segregation within buildings, the use of fire shutters and well-rehearsed arrangements to remove, segregate or otherwise protect valuable items. At the time of the fire at Windsor Castle in 1992, arrangements were quickly put in place for valuable artwork to be transferred to areas of the castle that were not affected by the fire.

When an event occurs, there will be a need to contain the cost of the event. For example, among the activities for minimizing costs associated with serious fires are detailed arrangements for salvage and arrangements for decontamination of items that have suffered water or smoke damage. Damage limitation and cost containment are important components of risk management and are related to disaster recovery and business continuity plans, as considered in Chapter 11.

Disruption to a theatre performance

The owner of a theatre has undertaken an assessment of the events that could cause disruption to the performance that evening. The events that could cause disruption include a power cut, absence of a key actor, substantial transport failure or road closures that delay the arrival of the audience, as well as the illness of a significant number of staff.

Having identified the events that could disrupt the performance, the owner needs to decide what to do to reduce the chances of one of these events causing the cancellation of the performance. It may be possible to take some immediate actions that will reduce the chances of a cancellation, but other measures to reduce the level of risk may require planning and/or capital investment.

PART II REVIEW

Checklist

The review of Part II sets out a checklist for risk assessment, which provides a list of four items that should be reviewed to confirm that appropriate risk assessment activities have been developed and implemented. The starting point for developing an appropriate approach to risk assessment is to complete a riskiness index, described in Chapter 1, and analyse the extent to which risk events could have a potential impact on finances, infrastructure, reputation or marketplace.

The overall objective of risk assessment activities is to ensure that the potential impact of the risks faced by the organization is fully understood. For some organizations, understanding the risks is a sufficient basis for delivering the passive requirements of the risk management initiative. Understanding the risks may be sufficient for compliance, assurance and decision-making activities.

When an organization has decided that the risk management initiative should be proactive and should improve the efficiency and effectiveness of strategy, tactics, operations and compliance, a different set of requirements is placed on risk assessment activities. The risk assessment of potential impacts can be recorded in a risk register, but the anticipated consequences and how to influence and manage those consequences represent a much more dynamic approach to risk management.

The output from a risk assessment exercise is often recorded in a risk register. There is a danger that a risk register becomes a static record of the output from the risk assessment. This may be less of a problem when the organization is undertaking risk management activities for passive reasons, but it is unsatisfactory if a more proactive approach is desired. If the organization is being more proactive in its approach to risk management, the output from the risk assessment needs to be developed into a risk action plan.

The checklist below is intended to focus on the priority risk assessment activities for an organization that is designing and implementing a comprehensive risk management initiative. It sets out the issues relevant to risk assessment that need to be clarified by the organization.

1. Describe the risk assessment structure and procedures that will be adopted in the organization, including details of the risk classification system, who will be involved in the assessment activities, the information that is required and how that information will be collected.

2. Identify the level of impact that would be significant for the organization and undertake risk assessment activities that identify and analyse the events with the potential to have a significant impact on finances, infrastructure, reputation and marketplace presence.

3. Determine the anticipated consequences of each of the significant risks identified and evaluate each risk in terms of the consequences for the strategy, tactics, operations and compliance activities of the organization, so that appropriate risk responses may be identified.

4. Calculate, to the extent that the available information allows, the efficiency and effectiveness of the existing controls in place, in order to decide whether the current level of risk is acceptable to the organization, taking into account business and legal requirements.

Case studies

Scottish Government: risk management

Ownership of risk

Risks should be identified at a level where a specific impact can be identified and a specific action or actions to address the risk can be identified. All risks, once identified, should be assigned to an owner who has responsibility for ensuring that the risk is managed and monitored over time. Risk owners, in line with their accountability for managing the risk, should have sufficient authority to ensure that the risk is effectively managed. Risk owners should ensure that the risk is escalated where necessary to the appropriate level of management.

Assessing risk

It is important to establish a clearly structured process in which both likelihood and impact are considered for each risk and that the assessment of risk is recorded in a way that facilitates monitoring and prioritization. Risk assessment should be recorded in a way that demonstrates clearly the key stages of the process. Documenting risk assessment creates a risk profile for the organization that:

- facilitates identification of risk priorities (in particular to identify the most significant risk issues with which senior management should concern themselves);
- captures the reasons for decisions made about what is and is not tolerable exposure;
- facilitates recording of the way in which it is decided to address risk;
- allows all those concerned with risk management to see the overall risk profile and how their areas of particular responsibility fit into it; and
- facilitates review and monitoring of risks.

Risk appetite

When considering threats, the concept of risk appetite embraces the level of exposure which is considered tolerable and justifiable should it be realized. In this sense, it is about comparing the cost (financial or otherwise) of constraining the risk with the cost of the exposure, should the exposure become a reality, and finding an acceptable balance.

It should be noted that some risk is unavoidable and may not be within the ability of the organization to completely manage it to a tolerable level. For example, many organizations have to accept that there is a risk arising from terrorist activity which they cannot control. In these cases, the organization needs to make contingency plans.

(Based on information on the Scottish Government website 2012.)

Cambridge NHS: risk assessment framework

Projects or services need to identify and assess potential risks to ensure effective management is in place, decisions are made taking account of these risks, and organizations maintain an optimal balance of risk, benefit and cost. Risk is inherent in all activity. Organizations should not be risk averse, but risk aware. In many cases the level of risk identified will be deemed acceptable as part of the overall impact of the project or service.

Types of risk

Examples of the types of risk that organizations might encounter and need to protect against include:

- corporate risks – operating within powers, fulfilling responsibilities, accountability to public;
- risks to reputation – quality of services, communication, patient experience;
- external risks – political, environmental, social, meteorological;

- clinical risks – associated with service standards, competencies, complications, equipment, medicines, staffing, patient information;
- health and safety risks – ensuring the wellbeing of staff and patients while providing or using services;
- business risks – associated with managing the affairs of the organization, human resources, information and IT, internal management, achieving objectives;
- risks to assets – security, protection, optimum use, maintenance, replacement.

Process for risk assessment

1 Set the context – for example, new vasectomy clinic in a community setting. Draw up and use a process map of the service to clarify what processes are involved and focus the risk assessment.
2 Identify hazards and risks – for example, risk of staff sickness, risk of poor ventilation in the clinic room. To identify risks think of what can go wrong – use 'What if' questions, for example:
   - What if the patient does not attend?
   - What if the records management system is not available?
   - What if the GPs don't refer to the service?
   - What if the ventilation system in the clinic fails?
   - What if the patient acquires an infection?
   - What if a member of staff goes on long-term sick?
   - What if the estimated cost of a project is wrong?
   - What if the directorate does not meet national standards in its area?

3 Identify causes and consider what is in place and/or what steps have already been taken to manage the risks.
4 Quantify risks, using the recommended consequence and likelihood matrix to determine the risk score.
5 Consider how to manage the risks – this will be driven by the risk score. High and extreme risks should be added to the organizational risk register.
6 Reassess what the potential risk level will be after the action plans have been completed and if this is unacceptable, further action is required.

7 Review the risk list and progress with action plans at each clinical governance meeting, and consider any changes to the service and any inherent new risks.

(Based on information on the Cambridge NHS Trust website 2012.)

Coventry Building Society: operational risk

Operational risk is the risk of loss arising from inadequate or failed internal processes, people and systems or from external events, including legal risks. These risks are managed as an integral part of the operation of each business unit. Management has a responsibility to understand how operational risk impacts the area of the business for which they are responsible and for putting in place controls or mitigating activities. The operational risk department ensures coordination of risk assessment and resulting control activities, reporting ultimately to the board risk committee.

New operational risks arose in 2010 following the merger with Stroud & Swindon, from the integration work required to migrate the information stored on Stroud and Swindon systems onto the framework used by the society. There are risks both in undertaking this exercise, for example data errors on transfer and also a risk that as a result of the scale of work required, resource will be distracted from managing the ongoing operation of the society in a challenging external environment.

A dedicated steering group has been set up to manage this project with responsibility of also highlighting the impact on business as usual activity. This steering group is chaired by the chief operating officer and updates from this steering group are provided monthly to the risk management committee and the board.

Financial crime is also recognized by the society as an evolving and substantial threat to the security and the safe operation of all financial institutions. The society continues to invest in monitoring and control systems to prevent increasingly sophisticated criminal attacks and has an excellent track record in this area.

The society has a duty of care to its staff, members and visitors while present on society premises. The society has in place comprehensive health and safety policies and a compliance regime which includes internal and external inspection, the maintenance and testing of equipment as well as appropriate training programmes; these are reviewed regularly. This work is overseen by the security and safety committee which reports to the risk management committee and the board.

In addition, the society has developed business continuity plans to manage situations in which buildings, systems or significant staff are unavailable, for example in the event of a flu pandemic or the loss of utilities. The business continuity plan is overseen by the operational risk and compliance committee and ultimately the board risk committee.

(Edited extracts from Coventry Building Society Annual Report and Accounts 2010.)

Further reading

BSI (2011) *British Standard BS 31100 (2011): Risk Management. Code of practice and guidance for the implementation of BS ISO 31000*, www.standardsuk.com

COSO (2004) *Enterprise Risk Management – Integrated framework, executive summary*, www.coso.org

Financial Reporting Council (2005) *Internal Control. Revised guidance for directors on the Combined Code*, www.frc.org.uk.

HM Treasury (2004) *Orange Book, Management of risk – principles and concepts*, www.hm-treasury.gov.uk

Hopkin, P (2012) *Fundamentals of Risk Management*, ISBN 978-0-7494-6539-1, Kogan Page: www.koganpage.com

Institute of Chartered Accountants in England and Wales (2002) *Risk Management for SMEs*, www.icaew.com

Institute of Risk Management (2002) *A Risk Management Standard*, www.theirm.org

Institute of Risk Management (2010) *Structured Approach to Enterprise Risk Management and the Requirements of ISO 31000*, www.theirm.org

PART III
Risk response

This component requires the organization to identify the nature of the controls that are in existence and/or additional controls that are required, as well as to consider the need for disaster recovery and business continuity plans.

Importance of risk response

Part III is concerned with the organization deciding on appropriate risk responses for the range of risks that it faces. The risk response component defines how the organization is going to design and implement suitable controls for the risks it faces and ensure adequate resilience of operations. Planning the risk response component starts with a consideration of the range of responses available, so that all risks achieve a level of risk that is tolerable for the organization. The risk responses are often referred to as terminate, treat, transfer and tolerate. This range gives rise to a variety of types of control that the organization can introduce. Consideration should be given to identifying the appropriate type(s) of control for an individual risk. The types of control available are:

- *preventive* controls that are designed to eliminate the possibility of the risk materializing and may be considered to be actions to terminate the risk;

- *corrective* controls that are designed to reduce the likelihood and magnitude of the risk and may be considered to be actions to treat the risk;
- *directive* controls that are based on directions or procedures that should be followed and may be considered to be actions to transfer the risk;
- *detective* controls that are based on identifying incidents after the risk has occurred and may be appropriate where the response to the risk is to tolerate it.

Part III considers practical examples of the various types of controls including the importance of insurance and transfer of risk by contract as risk control mechanisms. The development of a coordinated set of controls is also considered, including the development of a loss control initiative based on coordinated actions to achieve the initiative's three components, usually identified as loss prevention, damage limitation and cost containment.

An important consideration for all organizations is the resilience of their operational activities. Crises, disasters, unplanned disruption, as well as inefficient operations will occur from time to time. Organizations should ensure that suitable and sufficient plans are in place to cope with any unplanned disruption and/or dysfunctional operations. These actions will include the development and rehearsal of disaster recovery plans and business continuity plans.

The importance of risk response is reinforced by understanding the importance for the organization of identifying the critical controls that are in place to ensure satisfactory management of risks. If risk control improvements are required, a robust risk action plan should be developed. The efficiency and effectiveness of controls should be kept under constant review, so that the organization continues to learn from risk response activities.

Decisions about risk responses should ensure that the controls in place are always relevant and focused, and suitable and sufficient for the organization. In respect of the significant risks, the organization should always be aware of the level of risk that is present and the critical controls that are in place to make that level of risk tolerable. The level of risk is normally described by risk professionals as the combination of the likelihood of the risk event occurring and the potential impact.

Scope of risk response

The scope of risk response activities can be demonstrated by use of the risk management bow-tie. This simple diagram, shown in Figure PIII, extracts information from the risk management cube shown in Figure I in the Introduction. It incorporates the key messages relevant to effective and efficient risk response.

The risk response bow-tie illustrates that development of appropriate risk response activities depends on consideration of the potential impact of risk events on the finances, infrastructure, reputation and marketplace of the organization. Risk responses should be relevant to the anticipated consequences of these events for strategy, tactics, operations and compliance. Management will be more interested in identifying actions to cope with the anticipated consequences of risk events than the analysis of the potential impact of these events.

FIGURE PIII Risk response bow-tie

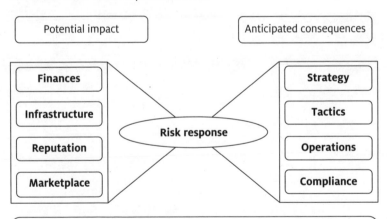

Key messages for Part III

Part III is concerned with risk responses and includes a consideration of the types of controls that are available to the organization. Appropriate controls need to be in place in all organizations to ensure that the current level of risk is tolerable. Actions will include implementation of appropriate controls that reflect the desired response of terminate, treat, transfer and tolerate by means of controls that are preventive, corrective, directive and detective; and evaluation of the need for enhanced resilience of the organization's operations by the design and implementation of suitable disaster recovery and business continuity plans.

CHAPTER NINE

RELEVANCE OF RISK RESPONSE

Purpose of risk response

Risk assessment is the activity of identifying all of the events that could have an impact on the organization. Having completed the risk assessment, the organization will have a list of risks and an analysis of the likelihood and potential impact of each risk, together with an evaluation of the anticipated consequences of each of the risks facing the organization.

Having undertaken the risk assessment, the organization will then need to respond to its findings. For some of the risks, the anticipated consequences will be within the willingness of the organization to take that particular risk. The willingness to take a particular risk may be related to the fact that the anticipated consequences are minimal or negligible. Also, a willingness to take a particular risk may be because it is considered that the risk is so unlikely to occur that it can be ignored.

Willingness to take a particular risk may be related to the fact that the risk is acceptable in terms of the potential rewards. Also, the risk may be within the risk criteria, risk appetite and/or risk capacity of the organization, depending on the terminology used and the overall approach to risk management. For the majority of risks where the potential impact could be significant, the organization will already have some controls in place so it may conclude that the current or residual level of the risk is acceptable and no further actions are necessary.

For organizations undertaking passive risk management, the outcome of the risk assessment exercise will be the analysis and evaluation of that particular risk. The organization will not be seeking to improve the level of risk performance, so it can be assumed that the current or residual level of risk is tolerable. A risk may be tolerable for a number of reasons, such as:

- the anticipated consequences should the risk materialize or the risk event occur would be minimal or negligible;
- suitable controls are already in place to the extent it is reasonably practicable, cost-effective and/or in compliance with legal requirements;
- the risk has been transferred or shared with a third party by means of insurance and/or contract terms and conditions;
- the risk is a business imperative that is inescapable given the existing business model and range of activities;
- the rewards available and/or received from the activities associated with that risk are sufficient to make the risk tolerable.

A good example of a tolerable risk was mentioned in Chapter 6: the broadcasting company that places a news team in a hostile part of the world. Another example may be when the manufacturer of products, such as motorcars, has decided to upgrade its product. The existing model may be selling well, but the organization knows that the long-term sales figures will be better if the models are kept up to date. Updating models may be high risk, both in terms of quality and timing, but the organization may still choose to have a schedule of routine updating.

In all cases, the organization will need to respond to the conclusions of the risk assessment. If an organization has a passive approach to risk management and is seeking compliance, assurance or risk management input into decision making, no further response would be required. However, if the organization has a proactive approach to risk management, it will wish to respond further to the output from the risk assessment and consider the introduction of further controls in the following circumstances:

- the current level of risk is deemed to be unacceptable;
- the introduction of further or additional controls is cost-effective;
- the level of risk has changed because of recent developments;
- more information is available about an emerging risk;
- stakeholder expectations have changed with regard to the risk; or
- improvements to efficiency and effectiveness are achievable.

Options for responding to risks

When the organization has completed the evaluation of the risks there are four possible ways in which it can respond, as follows:

1 *Terminate* – some risks will only be reduced to acceptable levels by terminating the activity. The option of termination of activities may be severely limited in government/public service organizations when compared to the private sector.

2 *Transfer* – for some risks the best response is to transfer them. This might be achieved by insurance, or by paying a third party to accept the risk in another way, such as contract. Transfer is particularly good for mitigating financial risks or risks to assets.

3 *Treat* – by introducing further controls to reduce risk likelihood and/or magnitude. The purpose of treatment is that, while the organization will continue with the activity giving rise to the risk, action is taken to control the risk to an acceptable level. This is the most common form of risk response.

4 *Tolerate* – the potential impact may be tolerable without any further action being taken. Even if it is not tolerable, the ability to do anything about some risks may be limited, and/or the cost of taking any action may be disproportionate to the potential benefit gained.

Different terminology is used for the different kinds of risk response. 'Tolerate' will often be described as 'accept' or 'retain' the risk. 'Treat' is often referred to as actions that are taken to control or reduce the risk. Transfer of risk is an important control measure for all organizations. The most common form of risk transfer is insurance; the importance of insurance as a control mechanism is considered in Chapter 10. Risk is also transferred by means of contract and this will be achieved by imposing specific contract terms and conditions.

An alternative term for 'risk transfer' is 'risk sharing'. Although this term is not as common, it is helpful to think about risk transfer being related to risk sharing because it is usually impossible to completely transfer a risk. The terms and conditions of an insurance contract will often make it clear that the insured party retains some of the risk. In a more practical sense, transferring a risk to a third party by contract may only be partially successful.

If a contractor fails to fulfil the contract, there may still be disruption to the counterparty. For example, failure of a supplier to deliver components to a car manufacturer will cause disruption to the production line. It is unlikely that the full cost of those production losses can be recovered from the supplier. This will be especially true if that supplier is a small company with limited resources and/or insurance.

The risk response 'terminate' is often referred to as 'avoid' or 'eliminate'. This response is only available in circumstances where the activity that gave rise to the risk is not a business imperative. Often, a manufacturing company will use component suppliers rather than manufacture the items itself and several activities may be outsourced. It might appear in these circumstances that the risk has been terminated, because it is no longer internal to the organization, but the risk still exists and if it materialized, it would still impact the organization.

To respond appropriately to a risk, the organization needs sufficient information about that risk. For example, a shop may consider that purchasing a small competitor only places the purchase cost at risk and the only control required is due diligence of the trading position of the target. In fact, it may be that the competitor is operating from premises built on contaminated land and the purchase of the business results in the purchaser acquiring the obligation to decontaminate that land. In this case, the purchaser did not obtain sufficient information and should have undertaken further investigations (due diligence) and possibly purchased insurance against the potential risk of acquiring the liability to decontaminate the land.

Selection of risk response

Generally speaking, a risk only becomes tolerable when all cost-effective control measures have been put in place, so that the organization is accepting or tolerating the risk at its current or residual level. Control measures may have been applied because the inherent level of the risk may have been unacceptable. Ultimately, the organization may decide to tolerate a particular risk. The example in the following box illustrates the range of risks that need to be considered. Successful risk responses need to be designed and implemented for each significant risk.

Example of risk versus reward

The current economic climate has made it very difficult for restaurants to survive. There appears to be an excessive number of restaurants compared with the customers available. The failure rate for restaurants is very high and research has shown that 60 per cent of restaurants fail within the first three years of operation.

Nevertheless, organizations and individuals are still looking to get into the restaurant business. This is because the rewards can be very high for successful restaurants: it has been estimated that 30 per cent net profit is achievable. The key risk factors that need to be evaluated are:

- Inadequate capital because the owner greatly underestimated how much it costs to open a restaurant and keep it running during the first few crucial months.
- Demanding workload and huge overtime hours. One restaurant owner and his partners spent well over 100 hours a week at work during the early days.
- Location has to be right, but choosing a location that is very popular for restaurants means the rent is likely to be higher and the competition stiffer.

Treatment is the most common response to risks. When a risk is high likelihood but low magnitude, the organization may decide to treat the risk, provided that this is cost-effective. Additionally, the organization may need to introduce further controls to be fully compliant with legal requirements. The risk treatment may reduce the likelihood of the event occurring and/or reduce the magnitude of the event when it does occur. Whether the approach to risk management is passive or proactive, the final result should be that the current level of risk becomes tolerable.

Transfer of risk is most common when the risk is high impact and low likelihood. Insurance is a well-established mechanism for transferring the financial impact of losses arising from infrastructure risks. In some cases, risk transfer is closely related to the desire to eliminate or terminate the risk. However, many risks cannot be fully transferred to the insurance market, either because of prohibitively high insurance premiums or because the risks under consideration have (traditionally) not been insurable and, therefore, no insurance products exist.

Risk transfer can be achieved by conventional insurance and also by contractual agreement. It may also be possible to find a joint-venture partner or some other means of sharing the risk. Risk hedging or neutralization may therefore be considered to be a risk transfer option, as well as a risk treatment and/or risk sharing option.

The response of terminate the risk is most appropriate when a risk is both of high likelihood and high potential impact. The organization will want to terminate or eliminate the risk. It may be that the risks of trading in a certain part of the world or the environmental risks associated with continuing to use certain chemicals are unacceptable to the organization and/or its stakeholders. In these circumstances, appropriate responses would be elimination of the risk by stopping the process or activity, substituting an alternative process or outsourcing the risky activity.

Implementing appropriate controls

Having decided the type of response that is appropriate, the organization will need to identify controls that deliver the type of response required (designing appropriate risk responses and controls is the subject of Chapter 10). The box below is an example of the way in which a combination of different controls is introduced to deal with a particular risk.

Reducing the chances of a player being absent

A sports club will want to reduce the chances of a key player being absent. The absence may be caused by inappropriate behaviour by a player, resulting in sanctions against that person. Accordingly, the club may decide to introduce a 'code of behaviour' for senior players; this would include a commitment by each player to follow an appropriate healthy lifestyle. Failure to comply with the code of behaviour would result in financial and other punishments.

The club may also decide that additional controls are required, including fitness monitoring and social support for overseas players who had recently moved to the country to join the team. It may also be agreed that an attempt should be made to place contractual limits on the ability of national teams to call on its overseas players. These actions will be taken in addition to other loss control activities, such as excellent medical facilities to provide immediate medical care and reduce the damage when an injury occurs. Also, the company may purchase insurance to protect itself against the financial losses associated with the absence of a player.

Whether the approach is passive or proactive, an analysis of the range of options available will be undertaken. When a passive approach to risk management is taken, the motivation is to have sufficient controls in place to ensure compliance and be able to provide assurance to relevant stakeholders. When a more proactive approach is taken, individual controls will be evaluated in terms of the benefit each control brings to the enhanced efficiency and effectiveness of strategy, tactics, operations and compliance. (The efficiency and effectiveness of controls is considered in more detail in Chapter 12.)

The important issue to consider when implementing appropriate controls is that the controls may not operate independently. In fact, it is possible to introduce a control to overcome a particular risk, but that control increases other related risks. For example, requiring operators to wear certain kinds of safety equipment, such as heavy safety clothing or safety goggles, may reduce overall mobility or visibility. This could result in an increase in the risks associated with restricted movement or limited vision. So, the controls that are selected and introduced should be viewed as a package of controls that need to work together. For this reason, some approaches to risk management recommend having an integrated approach to risk response. In simple terms, this will require an evaluation of every new control that is proposed to decide how effective it will be at reducing the risk being targeted compared with the possibility of increasing other risks.

CHAPTER TEN

DESIGNING RISK CONTROLS

Selection of controls

This chapter considers the types of controls that can be introduced when responding to individual risks. It is helpful to identify the type of control that is being introduced, because there is a hierarchy of controls – those at the top of the following list are likely to be more effective than those further down. The various types of controls can be described as:

- preventive controls designed to prevent the risk occurring and are related to the risk response 'terminate';
- corrective controls that reduce the likelihood and or potential impact of risks that do occur and are related to the risk response 'treat';
- directive controls that depend on instructions or directions on how to behave should the risk occur and are related to the risk response 'transfer'; and
- detective controls that identify circumstances when the risk has occurred and are related to the risk response 'tolerate'.

As with all classification systems, they may not be precise and or helpful in all circumstances. Also, there are certain controls that will be one type of control in certain circumstances and another type in slightly different circumstances. For example, validation of bank transfers by requiring two members of staff to independently login to the company bank account and authorize the transaction is designed to prevent fraud. If it is rigidly enforced, it may be considered to be a preventive control. However, this is more likely to be a corrective control that reduces the likelihood of fraud occurring, because the control would be defeated if there were collusion between two members of staff.

Perhaps the more important distinction when considering types of controls is to divide them into controls that are introduced before the event occurs and those that come into force after the incident. Preventive and corrective controls are designed to prevent the risk event occurring, although corrective controls will also act to reduce the likelihood and/or potential impact if the risk does occur. It is sometimes difficult to measure the effectiveness and efficiency of preventive and corrective controls, because there should be limited experience of the risks occurring.

Directive and, especially, detective controls are post-incident controls. Directive controls depend on the implementation of instructions or directives that have been given before the event, but need to be implemented after the event. The best examples of directive controls are those related to disaster recovery and business continuity plans. These represent a coordinated set of directions that should be followed if a specific event or set of circumstances occur. Transfer of risk by insurance or contract is a directive control, because the insurance or other contract will direct the parties as to how they should behave in the event of a loss.

It can, therefore, be seen that directive controls are not the strongest types of controls, because they depend on all parties being familiar with the requirements and acting as expected by the other party and as required by the contract. Breach of contract allegations, including breach of insurance contracts, are commonplace in business. Another example of the weakness of directive controls relates to the use of safety equipment. Safety equipment is only effective if it is properly maintained and used and this will not always be the case.

Finally, detective controls are also post-incident controls. These are described in more detail in the paragraphs that follow, but it is obvious that detective controls are based on identifying circumstances where the risk has occurred. These circumstances are then analysed, so that enhanced cost-effective controls to prevent the risk materializing again, perhaps with greater consequences, can be introduced.

Preventive and corrective controls

Preventive controls are designed to limit the possibility of an undesirable outcome being realized. The more important it is to stop an undesirable outcome, the more important it is to implement appropriate preventive controls. Corrective controls are designed to correct undesirable circumstances and reduce unacceptable risk exposures. Such controls provide a method whereby the risk is treated so that it becomes less likely to occur and/or the impact is much reduced. Corrective controls are designed to correct the situation, so machinery guards are corrective controls.

Examples of preventive controls include the separation of duty, whereby no person has authority to act without the consent of another when paying an invoice. Also, expenditure systems should prevent the same person from ordering goods and then authorizing the payment for those goods. In health and safety terms, preventive controls include the elimination or removal of the risk and substitution with something less risky. For example, a risky chemical used in a cleaning operation may be substituted with a less harmful one.

The advantage of preventive controls is that they eliminate the risk, so that no further consideration of it is required. In reality, this may not be a cost-effective option and may not be possible for operational reasons. The disadvantages of preventive controls are that beneficial activities that deliver rewards will be eliminated and either outsourced or replaced with something less effective and efficient.

Corrective controls are designed to limit the scope for loss and reduce any undesirable outcomes that have been realized. They may also be designed to achieve recovery against loss or damage. Examples of corrective controls can be found in the management of health and safety at work. Engineering containment by way of barriers or guards is a very well-established type of corrective control. In relation to fraud exposures, use of passwords or other access controls can be considered to be corrective controls. Staff rotation and regular change of supervisors also fit into this category of controls.

The advantage of many corrective controls is that they can be simple and cost-effective. Also, they do not require that existing practices and procedures are eliminated or replaced with alternative methods of work; the controls can be implemented within the framework of existing activities. The disadvantage of some corrective controls is that the marginal benefits that are achieved may be difficult to quantify or confirm as cost-effective.

Directive and detective controls

Directive controls are designed to ensure that a particular outcome is achieved. They are based on giving directions to people, or third-party organizations, on how to ensure that losses do not occur. They are important, but depend on people following established procedures. An example of directive controls is the requirement to wear personal protective equipment when undertaking potentially dangerous activities. Staff will need to be trained in the correct use of the equipment and a level of supervision will be required to ensure that it is used correctly.

The advantage of directive controls is that the risk control requirements can be explained during normal training and instruction sessions provided for staff. However, directive controls, especially in relation to health and safety risks, represent a low level of control that may require constant supervision.

Detective controls are designed to identify occasions of undesirable outcomes having been realized. Their effect is, by definition, 'after the event' so they are only appropriate when the organization is willing to tolerate the loss or damage that has occurred. Examples of detective controls include checks on stock or assets to ensure that they have not been removed without authorization. Bank reconciliation exercises can detect unauthorized transactions. Also, post-implementation reviews can detect the lessons learnt from completed projects. Detective controls are closely related to review and monitoring exercises undertaken as part of the risk governance activities in the organization.

The advantage of detective controls is that they are often simple to administer. In any case, they are essential in many circumstances where the organization will require early warning that other risk control measures have broken down. The disadvantage of the detective controls is that the risk has already materialized and is being detected after the event. However, it could be argued that the existence of the detective controls will deter certain individuals from attempting to defeat other risk controls.

Applying all four types of control to road safety

A road haulage company has decided to investigate the structure of preventive, corrective, directive and detective controls and what additional controls should be introduced to reduce the number of road accidents. The following controls have been identified:

1 *Preventive controls* include review of vehicle routing and realistic estimates of delivery times, so that drivers do not need to drive dangerously to arrive on time.

2 *Corrective controls* include enhanced maintenance procedures and improved arrangements for drivers to report vehicle defects.

3 *Directive controls* will be based on defensive driver training and the provision of an easy to understand vehicle driver handbook with practical advice.

4 *Detective controls*, by way of tachographs in the vehicles, are already used and it has been decided to also introduce regular checks of drivers' licences for penalty points.

These are just examples of some of the controls that the company has introduced. Other controls include routine inspections of vehicles to discover and report damage and review of fuel consumption to identify drivers with an aggressive driving style. The company has introduced a number of measurable loss control programmes to reduce the overall cost of running a fleet of vehicles.

Insurance as a control

Certain types of insurance contracts require the insurance company to pay for losses suffered directly by the insured. This is first-party insurance and includes property damage insurance. Other types of insurance require the insurance company to pay compensation to other parties if they have been injured or suffer loss because of the activities of the insured. This is third-party insurance and includes motor third-party and public/general liability.

The disadvantages of insurance include the delays often experienced in obtaining settlement of a claim and the difficulties that can arise in quantifying the financial costs associated with the loss. There may be disputes over the extent of the cover that has been purchased and the exact terms and conditions of the insurance contract. Also, the insured may have difficulty in deciding the limit of indemnity that is appropriate for liability exposures. This may result in under-insurance and the subsequent failure to have claims paid in full.

Insurance is a risk transfer or risk sharing response. It represents an after the event cost containment response to a risk. Insurance is most important for low probability high impact risks, such as destruction of assets or the payment of liability costs in circumstances where liability insurance is legally required and/or catastrophic losses are possible. As well as repairing assets, insurance is available for the cost of implementing disaster recovery and business continuity plans.

The most common reason for organizations to buy insurance is that it will protect the balance sheet and/or profit and loss account. Organizations also buy insurance when they are legally or contractually obliged to do so. In addition, there is increasing use of insurance to provide funding for employee benefits and/or the protection of employee assets. The latter is often achieved by the purchase of directors and officers liability insurance.

There is a wide range of different types of insurance available and the specific activities and features of the organization will help determine the scope of insurance that needs to be purchased. Sometimes, there is a shortage of insurance capacity and although the organization has decided that it wishes to purchase that type of insurance, it may not be available at an affordable cost.

Whatever type of insurance is being purchased, the organization will need to make decisions about how much insurance to buy and the most suitable company to use. The organization will need to consider the six aspects, frequently referred to as the six Cs of buying insurance:

1 *Cost* – the cost of insurance is the premium the organization has to pay plus the level of self-insurance (including the excess or deductible) that is imposed by the policy. This means that if a claim occurs, the organization will have to pay the first part of the claim before receiving any money from the insurance company.

2 *Coverage* – insurance policies usually have limitations, warranties and exclusions. These will state that claims will be refused in certain circumstances. These coverage issues need to be explored in detail by the organization buying the insurance to ensure that adequate coverage is available. The only reason for buying insurance is that claims will be paid when one of the identified events occurs.

3 *Capacity* – for very large organizations with considerable assets, one insurance company on its own may not be willing to offer coverage up to the full value of those assets. When buying insurance, the organization will need to think about the capacity the insurance company is willing to offer in relation to the value of the assets/ exposure that needs to be insured.

4 *Capabilities* – many insurance companies offer services in addition to insurance. These may include loss control services and assistance with business continuity planning. The capabilities of the insurance company in these areas may be an important factor in deciding which insurance company to choose.

5 *Claims* – the handling of insurance claims can be a detailed and forensic exercise. In risk management terms, depending fully on insurance to make good all losses is not sufficient. Every organization should look to its business continuity plans to ensure that arrangements are in place to guarantee minimum disruption should an adverse event occur.

6 *Compliance* – there is increasing concern about compliance issues in relation to insurance policies. Most countries have insurance premium taxes that must be paid to the appropriate national authority. Compliance issues also extend to the requirement to buy certain insurances in the local insurance market, issue policies in the local language and/or follow certain procedures in the event of a claim.

An example of insurance strategy

As with all risk responses, an organization should decide the appropriate cost-effective approach. The following is from the website of Royal Dutch Shell plc:

Shell mainly self-insures its risk exposures. Shell insurance subsidiaries provide insurance coverage to Shell entities, up to $1.15 billion per event generally limited to Shell's percentage interest in the relevant entity. The type and extent of the coverage provided is equal to that which is otherwise commercially available in the third-party insurance market. While from time to time the insurance subsidiaries may seek reinsurance for some of their risk exposures, such reinsurance would not provide any material coverage in the event of an incident such as BP Deepwater Horizon. Similarly, in the event of a material environmental incident, there would be no material proceeds available from third-party insurance companies to meet Shell's obligations.

CHAPTER ELEVEN

DISASTER RECOVERY AND BUSINESS CONTINUITY

Preparing for disruption

There has been a significant increase in interest in disaster recovery planning and business continuity planning. Together, these are often referred to as business continuity management. Whatever terminology is used, the aim is to increase the resilience of the organization when an event occurs that can cause significant unplanned disruption to normal activities.

In simple terms, the design, implementation and rehearsal of disaster recovery and business continuity plans are to ensure that the organization is in the best position to respond when an adverse event occurs. Therefore, these plans are 'after the event' plans. They are based mainly on instructions, or directions, given to members of staff and others on how they should respond when the event occurs. Disaster recovery and business continuity plans are therefore directive controls.

Disaster recovery and business continuity planning are related topics, each with a different emphasis. Disaster recovery planning is associated with coping with the immediate impact of a disaster. The most common reason for developing disaster recovery plans is related to the failure of a computer system. For organizations highly dependent on their computer systems, failure could result in total shutdown of business activities. For example, an online trading company would be unable to trade if it suffered a failure of its computer systems; the need to recover from such a disaster would be urgent and immediate.

Business continuity planning is subtly different. Staying with the example of computer systems, there would be a need to reinstate the failed computer as quickly as possible. While this was occurring, the organization would need to continue trading and this would be achieved through a business continuity plan.

When planning the scope of disaster recovery and business continuity plans, the organization should take an 'all-risks' approach. The exact cause of any disruption to an organization may be hard to identify and so it is important to focus on the key components or key dependencies within the organization that would result in severe disruption, if they were to fail. This analysis is usually referred to as 'business impact analysis', discussed below.

Example of disaster recovery planning

The printing industry has to respond rapidly to customer delivery schedules. Disruption to printing capability would have a major impact on customers and preparation of disaster recovery plans is vitally important. A typical approach to disaster recovery planning for a printing company would be as follows.

The disaster recovery plan provides a structured approach for responding to unplanned incidents that threaten our ability to conduct business in a timely manner. These include hardware, software, networks, people and buildings. Protecting our investment in our infrastructure and ability to conduct business is the key reason for implementing a disaster recovery plan.

The main components of the disaster recovery plan are:

- *Mirrored sites* – we have a fully mirrored site for use in the event of an incident at our main location and we can switch over to production at our alternative site within a matter of hours.
- *Stock replacement* – most of the stock that we hold can be easily replaced, although there are printed stock items that would take up to a week to replace. Our entire stock is fully insured.

- *Computer failure* – replacement of the computer hardware can be sourced within seven days and all hardware is fully insured.
- *Software replacement* – all programs are backed up and held off site and most software could be sourced within 24 hours.
- *Data back-up* – all data is backed up and stored off site. However, it would take up to a week to rebuild the systems, so a maximum of two days' data could be lost.

If a chain of retail shops had three distribution depots and one of them was destroyed by fire, the disaster recovery plan would be activated. This disaster recovery plan would overcome the immediate consequences of the fire, limit the damage by seeking to salvage damaged goods and minimize the immediate disruption to routine activities. The business continuity plan would represent the alternative arrangements put in place as the distribution centre was rebuilt. This would probably involve increased operating costs and these may be covered by the property damage insurance policy.

If a broadcasting company were to suffer a power cut at a broadcasting centre, there would be a need to recover immediately from this disaster. The disaster recovery plan would include alternative power supplies, such as generators and battery power. There may also be a need to temporarily locate to an alternative broadcasting facility. If the disruption to power was caused by serious damage within the building, a business continuity plan would be required such as taking over alternative broadcast facilities in a manner anticipated in advance by the plan.

Business impact analysis

To construct robust disaster recovery and business continuity plans, the organization needs to undertake a business impact analysis. This analysis will identify the critical nature of each business function by assessing the impact of interruption to that activity. The business impact analysis is similar to a risk assessment, except that the emphasis of the impact analysis is to identify the relative importance of each function, rather than identifying the events that could undermine that function. The business impact analysis has three clear purposes:

1. Identify mission-critical activities and the required recovery time in the event of disruption. This process will establish the timeframe within which the critical functions must be restored after the disruptive event.

2. Establish the impact potential and the resource requirements for recovery within the agreed timescale. The business requirements for successful recovery of the critical function must be established.

3. Determine whether the likely impacts are within risk tolerance, as the basis for the business continuity strategy. The technical requirements for recovery of the critical function also need to be established.

By identifying the sources of disruption that face the operations of an organization, undertaking a business impact analysis will become simpler. The focus of a business impact analysis, however, is likely to be on processes within the organization and how these may be disrupted. This seems especially relevant as continuity of business processes safeguards the interests of key stakeholders, reputation, brand and value-creating activities.

The example in the box below relates to the risks of cloud computing. Now that cloud computing has become commonplace, the need for individual organizations to prepare their own disaster recovery plan in the event of computer failure has changed. Organizations using the services of a cloud computing company are entitled to assume that back-up of their data is occurring in the cloud and alternative computing capacity will be made available by the organization providing the cloud computing facilities.

Although the responsibilities for disaster recovery and business continuity arrangements will be different when an organization uses a cloud computing company, the transfer of responsibility cannot be total. This is a good example of circumstances where there appears to have been a transfer of risk, but the reality is that the management of the risks related to constant availability of computing capability are now shared.

Risks of cloud computing

Previously, disaster recovery planning was applied mainly to actions to be taken in the event of a network computer failure. With the advent of cloud computing, the risk of a computer server failure has been transferred to the third party. However, as with all risk transfer mechanisms, the transfer can never be total.

Although the organization may not feel the need to develop detailed disaster recovery plans and may not need to arrange alternative computer facilities, certain risks remain. Set out below are just some examples of risks that need to be considered when placing an outsourced cloud computing contract:

- the arrangements may not achieve the anticipated cost savings;
- the working procedures may not suit the culture of the organization;
- there may be difficulty in integrating the cloud services provided;
- the solution may not comply with legal, contractual or moral obligations;
- a disaster may arise beyond the capability of the cloud provider;
- system privacy and confidentiality arrangements may be inadequate;
- system quality may be poor, so that it does not meet user needs.

Disaster recovery planning

Sometimes, a disaster will strike an organization in a way that is totally unexpected and the disaster develops so rapidly that detailed disaster recovery plans or crisis response plans have not been prepared. For this type of circumstance, it is likely that the organization will concentrate all of its efforts on managing the unexpected crisis that has arisen. Though the crisis may be unexpected, the organization should have put in place arrangements for responding to an unexpected crisis.

If the circumstances that have arisen are foreseeable, the organization should have developed detailed disaster response plans. Sometimes, crisis management will involve the use of alternative facilities that have been identified before the crisis arose. Plans that have been devised in advance will respond to the disaster, although it is not always possible to anticipate all disasters or predict how rapidly the crisis will develop and how serious it will ultimately become.

Unexpected disruption

The ash cloud from the volcano in Iceland in 2010 caused significant disruption to air travel and cancellation of many flights. Most organizations would not have foreseen disruption caused by an ash cloud nor planned appropriate actions for such an event.

However, disruption to travel patterns and the inability to fulfil travel plans are foreseeable business risks that can arise from a variety of causes. The challenge, therefore, is to respond to the risk of disruption to travel plans, rather than implement a plan specifically in response to an ash cloud.

Disaster recovery plans relate mainly to the damage limitation and cost containment components of loss control, as described in Chapter 8. A significant challenge for organizations is to identify the events that could occur that could disrupt normal efficient operations. Given this challenge, it is probably a better approach for the organization to concentrate on the loss of a vitally important component of the business, rather than trying to identify every cause that could result in a loss. Indeed, this is exactly the approach taken when undertaking a business impact analysis, as described earlier.

An important feature of disaster recovery plans is the protection of the reputation of the organization. When a major traffic accident occurs that causes the death of members of the public, a transport company involved in the crash would need to activate its disaster recovery plan. A substantial component of the plan will be arranging for a senior member of the organization to visit the scene and provide appropriate reassurance to customers, the media and other stakeholders. Likewise, when quality concerns are raised about a product, it could represent a disaster for the organization and it will need to respond accordingly.

Disaster recovery plans have to be communicated to staff and managers in advance of the event. Training in how to respond to the disaster is a critical component of successful disaster recovery planning. People with a defined role in the plan should be provided with necessary training and all members of staff should be trained so they can take appropriate protective actions during an emergency.

Implementation of the plans is vitally important so the organization needs to identify the resources required should the disaster materialize. The disaster recovery plan should include details of how to protect people, property and the environment during the disaster. Arrangements to communicate with customers and other stakeholders should also be in place to provide accurate information on the events that have occurred and the actions the organization has taken to manage them.

Business continuity planning

Business continuity plans build upon the disaster recovery plan by setting out longer-term plans for restoration of 'business as usual' in the immediate aftermath of a disaster. A business continuity plan is an important part of reducing the anticipated consequences of the disaster and will be part of the cost containment arrangements. In simple terms, business continuity plans identify how an organization intends to continue its normal business activities following a major disaster. The disaster could have a major impact on the reputation of the organization and failure to resume routine activities will make the situation even worse.

Some organizations take the view that business continuity planning should have three components:

1 The first response to any major event is to seek to recover from the event by implementation of a disaster recovery plan. As the disaster recovery plan is being implemented, the organization will need to consider management of the crisis. This will require effective communication with all stakeholders, so that the damage to reputation resulting from the incident is kept to a minimum;
2 The second stage of response after the disaster recovery plan is, therefore, implementation of the crisis management arrangements.

3 The third stage of the business continuity plan is to introduce the alternative operating arrangements, to the extent that this is necessary. If the impact of the disaster is only short term, it is unlikely that alternative arrangements for ensuring business continuity will be required.

An important component of disaster recovery and business continuity plans is that they are tested and rehearsed. The primary purpose of testing is to ensure that staff and managers are aware of the role they should play and the responsibilities they should fulfil. Rehearsal of the plans will bring clarity to the roles and responsibilities, as well as identifying weaknesses in the existing plans. In some circumstances, rehearsal of the plans may be a legal or customer requirement, such as fire evacuation drills. The case study for West Somerset Community College (see pp 135–136) provides a practical example of contingency and business continuity plans for an educational establishment.

An important part of testing the disaster recovery and business continuity plans is to validate the recovery times for critical components identified in the business impact analysis. The recovery time should be appropriate and achievable in practice. The fundamental question to be answered is whether the plans will work. Although testing and rehearsal of plans can be time-consuming and potentially disruptive, there are significant benefits to be gained and lessons to be learnt from undertaking routine testing and rehearsal activities.

Finally, it is important that the business continuity plan covers all the operations and premises of the organization to ensure that the plan can facilitate a complete resumption of normal business functions. It is also important that the plan is cost-effective and proportionate to the risk exposures. The business continuity plan must be practical and easily understood by staff and others who are involved in the execution of the plan. Overall, the plan must be effective in that it will recognize the urgency of certain business components or functions and identify responsibilities for ensuring timely resumption of normal work or the introduction of temporary alternative arrangements.

CHAPTER TWELVE

EFFICIENCY AND EFFECTIVENESS OF CONTROLS

Selecting appropriate controls

For organizations undertaking passive risk management, the efficiency and effectiveness of controls is only relevant to ensuring that mandatory obligations are fulfilled and assurance can be provided to relevant stakeholders. Nevertheless, the efficiency and effectiveness of controls is vitally important. Assurance that adequate standards of risk management have been achieved can only be provided when design and implementation of necessary controls can be clearly demonstrated.

The selection of appropriate controls and the satisfactory operation of those controls require that risk management roles and responsibilities are allocated and fulfilled, as described in Chapter 14. It is important that controls are operating as intended and the current level of risk is in accordance with the conclusions of the risk assessment exercise. Another important consideration is that only necessary controls are in place. These considerations are explored in the case study of Organate Foods set out in Appendix 1.

Decisions about appropriate controls should pay due regard to compliance requirements and to the elimination of unnecessary controls. Legal obligations, such as those relating to health and safety and money laundering, may result in organizations introducing controls that they would not otherwise have in place. Some organizations may over-interpret such legal obligations and introduce procedures that are unnecessarily complicated and cause considerable inconvenience and annoyance to customers and/or other stakeholders.

The example in the following box describes a situation where different controls will be required in different circumstances. Many of the controls necessary in a high risk situation, such as a jewellery shop selling expensive items, will not be necessary in a grocery store. This example illustrates that the selection of controls should be proportionate to the level of risk. The controls also have to be appropriate for the level of reward achieved from the activity that is being risk assessed.

Shop security standards

In a security-conscious jewellery shop, customers are allowed into the shop one at a time. They are recorded on CCTV as they wait to enter. Items are held securely, and customers are invited to ask to view specific items under the constant attention of the sales assistants. Of course, some customers are put off, but equally the shop suffers negligible rates of shoplifting.

Contrast this with a supermarket, where there are no barriers on entry and customers are allowed to handle all of the items. There is CCTV monitoring the shop and there are likely to be store detectives patrolling – but the object of the security is to deter rather than to prevent shoplifting. Shoplifting does occur, but at rates that are acceptable to the shop owners. Conversely, few potential customers are put off visiting the shop because of the measures.

The risk assessment undertaken by the organization will draw conclusions on the potential impact of certain events, such as a robbery at a shop. The impact will vary greatly depending on the value of the goods that are for sale. The controls that are selected should pay due regard to the management of the potential impact on the finances, infrastructure, reputation and marketplace of the organization. Also, the controls should be appropriate and relevant to the anticipated consequences of a robbery in terms of the overall success of the business strategy, tactics, operations and compliance.

Another feature relevant to the selection of controls is that they should be compatible with the nature of the organization. There is no point in selecting controls that are bureaucratic and require written records if they are not consistent with the way the organization normally operates. For example, keeping handwritten records of expenses will be incompatible in an organization that otherwise operates entirely with computerized records.

Maintaining the risk action plan

For organizations that are undertaking proactive risk management to improve the effectiveness and efficiency of strategy, tactics, operations and compliance, the selection of appropriate controls is vitally important. The risk action plan will be based on the risk register for the organization and may contain reference to the organization's risk appetite and/or the risk management criteria that have been established.

However, the important issue is that the risk action plan pays due regard to the rewards that the organization is seeking for taking the risks that have been identified, analysed and evaluated. The risk action plan for such an organization will include a description of the following:

- existing controls and their effect on the potential impact of the risk on finances, infrastructure, reputation and marketplace;
- risk improvement recommendations designed to reduce the potential impact of the risk should it materialize;
- benefits of implementing improvements for the anticipated consequences in relation to strategy, tactics, operations and compliance; and
- measurable risk management programmes that monitor risk management performance within the organization.

The measurable risk management programmes will be an integral part of ensuring that risk management activities are aligned with business success and embedded within business activities. These programmes will monitor risk performance in a way that is indicative of the key indicators that are fundamentally important for continued business success. In addition to the measurable risk management programmes, the organization should evaluate external risk indicators relevant to their organization and successful performance.

The importance of maintaining the risk action plan is discussed in Chapter 15, as well as in Chapter 14 on the risk architecture and protocols.

The organization should monitor its own risk performance as part of internal management. This will include keeping track of the lagging indicators, such as customer complaints, workplace accidents and fraud experience. The key message is that risks should not be managed in isolation from the context that gave rise to the risks. Risk management activities should contribute to the overall success of the organization, rather than represent a separate set of management activities with their own stream of management information, as illustrated by the quote in the box below.

Example of risk engagement

The following extract from the Network Rail website illustrates the proactive approach taken to risk management that also seeks active stakeholder involvement:

Third parties have a big role to play in investing in the rail network and Network Rail is the principal point of contact for customers and stakeholders (such as developers and funders) wishing to invest in the rail network infrastructure (also referred to as enhancement of the network). This might include building on a Network Rail station, or other property sites, or changing rail infrastructure to deliver a specified benefit.

We welcome proposals to enhance the network and will work proactively with customers and stakeholders to develop their ideas. We also need to manage potential risks to the operational railway and therefore must balance the proposed enhancements against our current operational business and existing customer and stakeholder requirements. The earlier that Network Rail is involved in the development of a project, the greater focus we can give to influencing its scope and facilitating its delivery. While this will make the proposal more likely to be compatible with our existing obligations, it can also add value to the proposed output by providing a robust assessment of any interface risks with our existing operation, maintenance and renewal activities.

The organization should also monitor external indicators that could be indicative of emerging risks. These may be lead indicators that give early warnings that specific risks are more likely to materialize. For example, an organization that faces significant credit financial risks will monitor economic growth predictions and corporate bankruptcies. An organization facing significant market financial risks will monitor relevant interest rates and foreign exchange rates.

By maintaining the risk action plan in this way and keeping the contents of the plan dynamic, the organization will enhance its chances of success and, at the same time, ensure that risk management activities are aligned and embedded and contribute to the success of the organization. Monitoring of external lead indicators and responding to movements will ensure that risk management activities are dynamic within the organization. This approach to risk management represents a significantly more proactive approach than simply preparing a list of risks set out in a risk register for governance and assurance purposes.

The tracking of external lead indicators should provide the organization with early warning of emerging risks, as well as an indication that further analysis of potentially catastrophic high impact, low likelihood risks should be undertaken. The overall intention is to enhance the contribution that risk management makes to the success of the organization by anticipating adverse events. An even more proactive approach that builds on risk management is to use the information from these external leading indicators as a means of identifying strategic, tactical, operational and compliance opportunities.

Learning from controls

Figure 12.1 illustrates the steps involved in learning from controls. The overall approach can be described as plan – implement – measure – learn. This is consistent with the steps that would be taken when designing and implementing the overall risk management initiative. It also describes the four types of competency required by those involved in the planning and implementation of the initiative. To be successful, the initiative will require the involvement of individuals who are competent to:

- plan the risk management initiative;
- implement the activities that have been planned;

FIGURE 12.1 Learning from controls

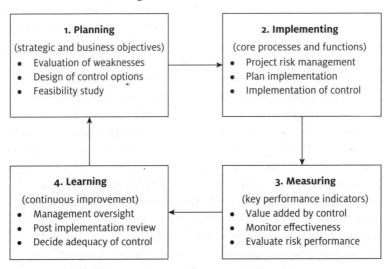

- measure the results of implementing those activities; and
- learn from the above and repeat the cycle.

Controls should be reviewed on a continuing basis, and Figure 12.1 shows a way of undertaking the continuous review that should be part of learning from controls. This constant review will result in a number of benefits. It will ensure that the controls are effective in producing the result that is required and controlling the risk to the standard that is set out in the risk management manual. Also, the efficiency of the existing controls can be evaluated, so that it can be decided whether the current level of control is achieved in a cost-effective manner.

Another important advantage of seeking to learn from controls is that any unnecessary and inappropriately complex controls will be identified and steps can be taken to remove, modify or replace them with more cost-effective options. Risk assessment activities should take account of the continuing review of controls that is taking place, because the level of risk will be affected by the nature and quality of the controls.

When undertaking any of the activities involved in learning from controls, it is important to keep in mind that the controls are the primary means by which the risk management initiative achieves the intended benefits. If the controls are in place as part of risk governance, then the primary driver will be to make the controls as efficient as possible. However, if the intention is to achieve enhanced efficiency and effectiveness of strategy, tactics, operations and compliance, a more business aware, cost-effective and/or risk to reward approach to controls is required.

Controls need to be appropriate for the level of risk faced by the organization. Deciding the level of risk will be the output from the risk assessment process, as well as being an output from completion of the riskiness index described in Chapter 1. The evaluation of the risks will be influenced by the risk agenda for the organization. The risk agenda will pay full regard to all of the factors affecting the organization, including stakeholder expectations.

Organizations operating in highly regulated business sectors should pay regard to the experiences of other organizations operating in the same sector. The case study at the end of this section refers to the BG Group plc Annual Report and Accounts 2010 (see pp 136–137). This extract provides information on how BG Group responded to the circumstances of the BP Macondo blow-out in the Gulf of Mexico in 2010, often referred to as Deepwater Horizon. This is an important extract from the Annual Report and Accounts because it demonstrates that learning from controls involves monitoring the experiences of other organizations, including competitors, operating in the same sector.

PART III REVIEW

Checklist

The checklist for risk response provides four items that should be reviewed to confirm that appropriate risk response activities have been developed and implemented. The starting point for developing an appropriate approach to risk response is to complete a riskiness index described in Chapter 1 and analyse the extent to which risk events could have a potential impact on finances, infrastructure, reputation or marketplace.

The overall objective of risk response is to ensure the selection of appropriate controls that are capable of providing assurance regarding risk management activities, as well as delivering a more proactive approach. The organization needs to develop a risk response for each type of risk that has been identified. Appropriate controls then need to be selected; broadly these are preventive, corrective, directive and detective controls.

When planning further risk management activities, the organization should pay regard to the current level of riskiness embedded within the organization. This is the basis from which the organization can build a more proactive approach to risk management. The proactive approach will seek to improve the efficiency and effectiveness of strategy, tactics, operations and compliance.

The checklist below is intended to focus on the priority risk management activities for an organization that is designing and implementing a comprehensive risk management initiative. The checklist sets out the issues relevant to risk response that the organization needs to clarify.

1 Determine the appropriate response to each of the significant risks identified during the risk assessment exercise, in terms of the willingness to tolerate the risk; the desire to treat the risk by modifying existing controls; the availability of means to transfer the risk; and/or the desire to terminate the risk.

2 Identify the efficiency and effectiveness of existing controls to determine whether there is an urgent need to introduce further controls, and the nature of any additional controls in terms of preventive, corrective, directive and detective controls.

3 Undertake analysis and evaluation of the existing arrangements to cope with major disruption to the infrastructure of the organization and determine the need for rehearsal, review and/or enhancement of existing disaster recovery and business continuity plans.

4 Conduct a review to identify the critical controls in place in the organization and determine the efficiency and effectiveness of these controls, to enhance the controls, as necessary, and challenge any presumptions about the controls that were made in the risk assessment exercise.

Case studies

BBC: high risk policy

The BBC has special arrangements in place for high risk work. This includes deployments to hostile environments, undertaking activities such as covert filming of dangerous groups, and covering events such as terrorist incidents, natural disasters or pandemic diseases. The high risk guidelines apply to all of the following:

- BBC and independent productions commissioned by the BBC;
- BBC divisions, including commercial divisions, World Service, BBC Monitoring and the World Service Trust;
- BBC contracted staff and freelancers working on BBC projects, or sub-contractors and consultants engaged by the BBC;
- co-productions where the BBC is funding the major share of investment in the production.

Key requirements

Those undertaking or commissioning high risk work are required, as far as practicably possible, to:

- seek information and advice from the high risk team;
- complete a written risk assessment and apply the necessary safety control measures;
- ensure those involved have the right training and/or experience for the assignment;
- identify and use appropriate safety equipment;
- make adequate contingency plans and arrangements in case of emergency;
- obtain the appropriate level of management authorization.

Information and advice

Individuals should research the relevant background information (political, social, religious, military, etc) to the area or country in which they will be working. Useful sources are BBC correspondents, news resources, the language services of the BBC World Service, as well as external bodies and specialists. All staff planning high risk work should, where practically possible, first seek advice from the high risk team.

The high risk team maintains a schedule of 'hostile environments' and designates other areas 'travel advisory' on the BBC intranet which is regularly updated in consultation with regional bureaux. Countries listed as 'hostile environment' require the special provisions in these guidelines to be applied.

These guidelines do not apply to places listed as 'travel advisory', but staff unfamiliar with these places should contact the high risk team for advice. The high risk team will assist with the risk assessment process and provide advice on how to minimize risks, including:

- recommended methods of operating;
- individual and team security measures;
- protective equipment, first aid and trauma equipment;
- safety communications;
- contingency planning;
- remind staff of the need for preventive health measures.

(Based on information on the BBC website 2012.)

West Somerset Community College: contingency and business continuity

Potential disruptions

1. Loss of premises

Minehead is situated within a floodplain and it is a dense urban area and as such the watercourses have been culverted, modified and largely encroached upon by development. Currently 1,000 properties are in the 1 per cent annual probability event flood outline. Many agencies have worked in partnership to develop the local catchment flood management plan.

2. Loss of utilities

Emergency telephone numbers for use in the event of loss of utilities are supplied to key members of staff.

3. Virtual teaching

If there is a serious disruption to education, work can still be submitted by students and accessed by teachers via the college website.

4. Loss of communication

In the event of total loss of telecommunication, mobile phones and walkie-talkies can be used until the telephone system is repaired/replaced. In the event of replacement computers being required, the college will contact main suppliers and assess which contractor can replace equipment at the quickest/cheapest rate. The emergency contact arrangements for the network, service infrastructure and internet service provider are available from the college IT support team.

5. Loss and back-up of data

Servers at the college site hold all data and in the event of total loss it will be necessary to restore data from the last backup. Data on these servers is separately backed up daily and stored on a server in the administration block and a tape drive in the server room; tapes are then removed and stored in a fireproof safe. Tapes are reused on a rotational basis. In the event of loss of data, it can be recovered from the time of the last back-up.

6. Industrial action

As far as possible, without attempting to influence the legal rights of staff members to take industrial action, managers should try to estimate the proportion of staff that may be available to work in order to plan work in accordance with priorities.

Recovery

Long-term recovery may be affected by decisions made during the assessment and/or containment phase, so recovery issues should be taken into account by the department from the outset. Dependent on the nature of the incident, recovery may take months or even years to achieve (for instance if a full rebuild is required after a fire, or if injuries or deaths occur) and will include ways of keeping the academy community together during any period of dispersion.

(Based on information on the West Somerset Community College website 2012.)

BG Group: evolving risk profile

BG Group's risk profile continually evolves over time as a result of changes in both the external environment and the continued growth and development of the group's portfolio. For example, while BG Group's move into unconventional resources in the USA (shale gas) and Australia (coal seam gas) provides the group with significant growth opportunities and reduces the group's overall exposure to non-OECD countries, it also brings new risks and uncertainties that need to be managed.

World economy – economic conditions remain challenging for many OECD countries, including the USA. Although certain regions are demonstrating a return to economic growth, with emerging economies in Asia and South America showing strong momentum, there remains the risk that continued economic weakness or a return to economic uncertainty adversely impacts the demand for gas and oil which in turn could have an adverse impact on BG Group's business. BG Group's operations in North Africa have not been materially affected by political events in that region to date, although the group will continue to monitor developments carefully.

Safety and asset integrity – the BP Macondo blow-out in the Gulf of Mexico was a stark reminder that, in the oil and gas industry, there is an inherent potential for loss of life, environmental damage, and a consequential erosion of shareholder value from a single catastrophic event. It also brought into sharp focus the issue of how operators manage and communicate with their contractors and joint venture partners.

A failure to build, operate, maintain and decommission facilities in a safe manner in any environment could result in loss of life, production and revenues, cause significant damage to reputation or the environment and, ultimately, lead to an erosion of shareholder value.

In particular, the group is focused on contractor management and seeks to ensure that its contractors and joint venture partners adopt a safety culture and comply with safety standards that are at least equivalent to those applied by BG Group to its own operations. In response to the BP Macondo blow-out, BG Group has established a team to ensure lessons learnt from the incident are applied appropriately to its business. BG Group is involved with relevant industry bodies and intends to play its part in shaping the response of the industry as a whole.

Project delivery – the group's growth plans for the next decade are increasingly dependent on the successful development and operation of its existing projects, in particular its unconventional gas plans in Australia and the USA, and the group's interests in the deep-water oilfields in the Santos Basin, offshore Brazil. Each of these projects is inherently complex and their successful development remains a significant challenge for the group. As a result, the board and GEC receive regular updates on the management of these projects.

Capital expenditure – given the scale of BG Group's investment over the coming years – a period in which projects in Australia, Brazil and the USA will require significant capital expenditure – the board also remains focused on ensuring that the group remains soundly financed.

(Edited extract from BG Group plc Annual Report and Accounts 2010.)

Further reading

BSI (2011) *British Standard BS 31100 (2011): Risk Management. Code of practice and guidance for the implementation of BS ISO 31000*, www.standardsuk.com

COSO (2004) *Enterprise Risk Management – Integrated framework, executive summary*, www.coso.org

Financial Reporting Council (2005) *Internal Control. Revised guidance for directors on the Combined Code*, www.frc.org.uk.

HM Treasury (2004) *Orange Book, Management of risk – principles and concepts*, www.hm-treasury.gov.uk

Hopkin, P (2012) *Fundamentals of Risk Management*, ISBN 978-0-7494-6539-1, Kogan Page: www.koganpage.com

Institute of Chartered Accountants in England and Wales (2002) *Risk Management for SMEs*, www.icaew.com

Institute of Risk Management (2002) *A Risk Management Standard*, www.theirm.org

Institute of Risk Management (2010) *Structured Approach to Enterprise Risk Management and the Requirements of ISO 31000*, www.theirm.org

PART IV
Risk
communication

This component requires the organization to establish roles, responsibilities and communication procedures for risk management, as well as evaluate the requirements for a risk register and/or other form of risk action plan.

Importance of risk communication

Part IV is concerned with risk communications, both internal and external. The risk communication component is delivered by the organization's risk architecture, strategy and protocols. Adequate risk communication also requires that a suitable risk register and/or risk action plan is established by the organization. Implementing the risk communication component includes considering the need for the organization to prepare formalized policy statements and protocols for the management of risk information.

An organization should develop the risk architecture, strategy and protocols appropriate for the size, nature and complexity of the organization. This may include:

- a risk management policy statement of the overall intention of the organization with respect to risk management;
- statement of risk management roles and responsibilities for both individuals and the committees within the organization;
- risk management rules and procedures, including details of risk training, risk assessments, delegation of authority and risk escalation; and
- risk monitoring arrangements, including confirmation of the risk-related performance indicators that will be reviewed by top management.

Part IV also considers the management of risk information within an organization. Many organizations produce a risk register containing a list of the significant risks they face, but simply making lists is insufficient to improve the management of risk. The organization also needs to measure risk performance and monitor the efficiency and effectiveness of controls. This can be undertaken on an informal basis, although the most successful risk management initiatives will include the use of risk-related performance indicators that are integral to the success of the organization.

Risk communication protocols should also include details of risk management reporting. This is a fundamentally important requirement that includes both internal communications and external reporting. Internal communications will include risk escalation procedures and, in appropriate circumstances, whistleblowing arrangements. Risk reporting requirements are mandatory for many organizations, including charities, companies listed on stock exchanges, local and central government departments, as well as government agencies.

Communication of risk information is vitally important within all organizations. Many decisions are taken on the basis of a risk versus reward analysis and such decisions can only be undertaken if the risks are fully understood. In large organizations, risk communication arrangements will be more complex and formalized. This is also the case in all types of government establishments and departments.

In many organizations, a risk register will be produced and discussions will be held at an appropriate senior management committee. It is important to remember that the production of a list of risks with details of the controls that are in place does not automatically result in improved management of risk. When an organization is undertaking risk management activities for proactive reasons, a risk action plan will be more appropriate and effective than a static risk register.

Scope of risk communication

The scope of risk communication can be demonstrated by use of the risk management bow-tie. This simple diagram, shown in Figure PIV, extracts information from the risk management cube shown in Figure I in the Introduction. It incorporates the key messages relevant to effective risk communication.

The risk communication bow-tie illustrates that development of appropriate risk communication activities needs to consider the potential impact of risk events on the finances, infrastructure, reputation and marketplace of the organization. Risk communication should also ensure that the organization successfully focuses risk management attention on the anticipated consequences of these events for strategy, tactics, operations and compliance. Communication and sharing of risk information is critically important if management is to understand the

FIGURE PIV Risk communication bow-tie

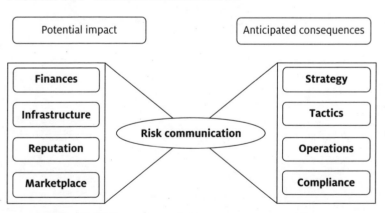

Potential impact

Anticipated consequences

Finances		Strategy
Infrastructure	Risk communication	Tactics
Reputation		Operations
Marketplace		Compliance

Key risk communication actions:
- Establish the risk architecture, strategy and protocols for the organization
- Produce a dynamic risk register describing critical controls and further actions

anticipated consequences of risk events and receive assurance that appropriate actions are being taken.

Key messages for Part IV

Part IV is concerned with internal risk communication and external risk reporting. The level of risk communication that is required will depend on the size, nature and complexity of the organization. However, in all cases risk information will need to be communicated within the organization and/or with external stakeholders. The following actions will be necessary: establish the risk architecture, strategy and protocols for the organization and produce these in writing to the extent that is appropriate to achieve adequate internal risk communication and to facilitate external risk reporting; and produce a dynamic risk register and/or risk action plan that includes details of critical controls and further actions that are required, ensuring that the information is fully aligned with the success of the organization.

CHAPTER THIRTEEN

RELEVANCE OF RISK COMMUNICATION

Nature of risk communication

Risk communication within an organization is essential if adequate management of risk is to be achieved. The organization needs to decide who will receive risk information; what risk information is going to be communicated; and how it will be communicated. This section considers these three questions, as well as a commentary on the broader issue of how risk management information is recorded and managed within the organization.

Chapter 15 considers the importance of the risk architecture and protocols for the organization; this includes information on the contents of a comprehensive risk management manual. Chapter 16 considers, in detail, the important role to be played by the risk register for the organization and how this can be developed into a risk action plan. Communication of risk information will need to take place internally within the organization, as well as externally to regulators and other stakeholders.

Regardless of whether the information is communicated internally or externally, the four main reasons for communicating risk information are:

1 part of governance arrangements and records, including the need to provide assurance to relevant stakeholders regarding risks and risk management activities within the organization;

2 part of tracking the status of the significant risks facing the organization, so that information on potential risk exposures can be used for enhanced decision making;

3 part of the means by which improvements in risk performance will be recorded and monitored, for organizations taking a proactive approach to risk management;

4 part of risk awareness and risk management training, including the need to communicate risk information to ensure appropriate and consistent behaviours and responses to risk, both internally and externally.

Risk information will be recorded and communicated by an organization in a number of different ways, depending on the nature of the information, the reason for communication and the audience. To be effective, the organization should establish mechanisms for risk information to be communicated within the organization and reported to external stakeholders. It is also important that mechanisms are established for the organization to collect and evaluate risk information, both internally and externally.

When establishing risk communication arrangements, consideration of stakeholders and their expectations is vitally important (the relevance of stakeholder expectations to the governance arrangements in the organization is considered in more detail in Chapter 20). For some organizations, stakeholders will include society in general and pressure groups in particular. Pressure groups can have a significant impact on the reputation of an organization and the need to communicate with such groups may be a critical component of the overall risk communication arrangements. This will be the case even when the board or executive committee is not in sympathy with the aims and objectives of the particular stakeholder pressure group.

The starting point for an organization planning its risk communication strategy is to decide how information on the risk agenda is recorded and communicated. The risk agenda is defined by an analysis of why the organization undertakes risk management activities and how they will be undertaken. The communication of risk information should be relevant to the success of the organization. This will be the case whether the risk agenda is based on passive reasons for undertaking risk management or a more proactive approach.

Risk management documentation

The size, nature and complexity of an organization will define the level of risk management documentation that is required. If necessary, the organization will produce a detailed risk management manual (described in more detail in Chapter 14). The nature of the risk management documentation will be influenced by the organization's risk agenda and whether it is a passive or proactive approach, and the extent of the documentation will be influenced by the level to which the organization is regulated.

Risk management documents will, broadly speaking, divide into two different types. First, there will be static documents that describe the risk architecture and protocols for the organization; second, there will be dynamic management reports that describe the current status of risk and risk management within the organization. These will include governance reports and performance reports related to measurable risk management programmes or initiatives.

The static risk management documents will include information related to risk management administration and governance. The risk register will be a static risk management document for organizations undertaking risk management for passive reasons. Dynamic risk management documents will include the risk action plan, reports of investigations of risk events and information on the performance of the various risk management initiatives. (Risk management reports and records are considered in more detail in Chapter 14.)

Some organizations will create committees that are exclusively concerned with risk and risk management issues and these will require their own terms of reference. Terms of reference will need to be produced for the audit committee and, if the organization has one, the disclosures committee. In some organizations, risk management is one of the responsibilities of a committee that has broader responsibilities. For example, it may be proportionate for a small company to have risk management as one of the responsibilities of the executive committee.

The results of a risk assessment exercise will normally be recorded in a risk register and this may be a static document in many organizations. (A more detailed evaluation of the development and use of risk registers is set out in Chapter 15.) Risk response documents include business continuity management plans prepared in advance that describe the actions to be taken if a specific event occurs. These risk response plans include disaster recovery and business continuity plans.

Documents that record the results of the investigation of events should also be kept. When a significant event occurs, the organization should record details of the circumstances and consequences of the event. Such reports may be required by the regulator, as well as being useful in the event of an insurance claim and/or contractual dispute. Event reports will also include information on, for example, customer complaints as well as records of other key performance indicators. These will be dynamic risk management documents.

Performance and certification reports may sometimes be required and these will include records of internal audit investigations. Regulations in some countries require that certain risk management processes, especially reporting processes, are reviewed by external auditors. This will result in reports that attest or confirm that the processes are suitable and sufficient. Also, the results of any self-certification procedures that the organization has introduced will need to be kept. Risk performance reports may also be required by regulators and could be required as part of external disclosure reports to a range of stakeholders.

Scope of risk documentation

In addition to the risk policy, the main risk management document is the risk register. This is primarily for reporting to management and may well be too detailed for the board. The board and the audit committee will have to determine how risk matters should be reported and how frequently.

The frequency of risk reporting to the board varies between organizations. Some have a standing item consisting of a short progress update against key risks and this might generally be considered to be good practice. Others ask for detailed reports on one of the major board level risks at every audit committee meeting and many have risk management as a permanent item on the agenda. Another approach is to have quarterly reports to the governing body as part of the review of strategic, tactical, operational and compliance performance.

In addition, a board should at a minimum receive – and approve – an annual risk report (usually prepared by the audit committee) that notes progress on all key identified risks. This is essential for internal purposes, and will form part of its compliance reporting to the stakeholders.

For risk management activities to be proactive, they need to be aligned with other activities, embedded within them and dynamic to changing circumstances. To be aligned and embedded, it is important that risk management documents are relevant to business priorities. In simple terms, it is important that risk management documents do not represent a separate stream of management information; this would reduce the influence of risk management activities, even those being undertaken for passive reasons.

Risk information and risk training

Risk management awareness should be embedded in all training, super-vision and instruction activities within an organization. For example, when a member of staff is being trained to undertake a specific task, the health and safety and other risk management considerations relevant to that task should be incorporated in the training. In some circum-stances, it is valuable to provide additional training that emphasizes risk management considerations. For example, an organization may decide to reinforce the quality awareness of employees by providing specific quality assurance training additional to the standard quality instructions embedded within on-the-job training.

Risk training is a key part of learning and communication and it is essential for the engagement of managers, staff and other stakeholders. It should cover a wide range of topics and achieve a greater understand-ing of all the risk-related issues, as well as providing information on the control measures that are in place and the vital role played by staff in the successful implementation of those controls. Post-training vali-dation should normally be undertaken to ensure that attendees are working in accordance with the issues discussed during their training courses. Records of risk training should be kept by the organization.

Risk training is an integral part of internal risk communication and will be a reflection of the organization's risk culture and level of risk maturity. The provision of risk training is a key component in achieving a high level of embedded risk management. Internal risk communica-tion is a broader topic than simply risk training and is considered further in Chapter 15. It is not usual for risk training to be provided to external stakeholders, but other means of risk communication are vitally impor-tant. The importance of external risk reporting is considered further in Chapter 16.

The provision of risk training should be aligned with other training activities within the organization. As with all other types of training, the content of the risk training must be consistent with the requirements of the job. Training on risk matters will be required in a number of circumstances, including:

- when new risks have appeared or existing risks have changed significantly;
- when an individual takes a new job or assumes additional responsibilities;
- after an incident has occurred to communicate the lessons learnt; and
- when new or enhanced procedures are introduced.

The box below provides a practical example of the relevance of risk management training in a publishing company and the way in which risk awareness needs to be embedded into the routine operations of the organization. In this example, the training activity is aligned with the main business activities of the organization, and the overall approach to risk management is that it is a facilitator of the activities of the organization and contributes to business success.

Risk training for journalists

A magazine publisher wishes to be known as a provider of high quality and accurate journalism. However, it has recently been successfully sued for libel, so the organization has decided that the libel and slander risk requires greater attention with a high profile set of risk guidelines, including awareness training for all staff.

Enhanced risk control standards for libel and slander are planned and these procedures will reflect the level of risk exposure. The nature of the attention paid to libel and slander risks will depend on each magazine title and the following framework has been agreed:

- all journalists to be given basic libel and slander training;
- specific review procedures introduced for political titles;
- legal evaluation of every issue of the satirical magazine.

Training has been provided for staff on the revised procedures and information has been included on the company intranet site. Managers and staff have been encouraged to comment on the new procedures, so that they may be improved further as part of the learning culture within the company.

Government risk communication

Risk communication is a potential concern for all types of organizations. It is, perhaps, at its most complex and challenging when it is a sovereign government that is seeking to communicate on risk issues. Government will be aware of the fact that people face a range of risks, including direct threats, risks to their safety, welfare or livelihood, as well as concerns about risks to the environment. However, government has a dual role in relation to risk communication that may, in many instances, result in difficulties in communicating on risk issues.

It is clear that the role of government will vary according to the nature of the risk. This role may involve providing information and advice to individuals on risks that they manage themselves. For example, the risks associated with obesity need to be communicated by government, but the management of these risks is primarily reliant on the behaviour of individuals. Nevertheless, government will be concerned about the risks to society and government finances that are associated with obesity.

Government needs to balance the requirements of society as a whole with the concerns of different stakeholder groups. A stakeholder group may be concerned about the health and safety risks associated with, for example, a domestic waste incinerator that is being built in the vicinity. Government advisers may be convinced that the risks to public health are minimal but their assurances may not be accepted by local pressure groups.

Accordingly, government needs to establish a set of principles for communicating on risk matters with the general public. The UK government has stated that the following five principles should apply to the handling of all types of risk to the public:

1 *Openness and transparency* – Government will be open and transparent about its understanding of the nature of risks to the public and about the process it is following in handling them.
2 *Involvement* – Government will seek wide involvement of those concerned in the decision-making process and actively involve significant stakeholders throughout the risk identification, assessment and management process.
3 *Proportionality and consistency* – Government will act proportionately and consistently in dealing with risks to the public and will base all decisions about risks on what best serves the public interest.
4 *Evidence* – Government will seek to base decisions on the consideration of all relevant evidence and ensure, where possible, it is quantified before decisions on risk are taken.
5 *Responsibility* – Government will allocate responsibility for managing risks to those best placed to control them and ensure that those who impose risks on others have responsibility for control and the consequences of inadequate control.

Although this example is related to communication of risk information by government, it demonstrates the importance of risk communication generally and the need for an organization to clearly establish the reasons for communicating risk information; the stakeholders who are entitled to receive it; and, most importantly, the nature and extent of the information communicated.

CHAPTER FOURTEEN

RISK ARCHITECTURE AND PROTOCOLS

Risk management manual

The range of risk management documentation that may be held by an organization is described in Chapter 13. The most important risk management documents will be collected together in the risk management manual. It should set out the key features of the risk agenda by describing the risk architecture, strategy and protocols for the organization. To be successful in driving risk management, the policy should be fully aligned with the management priorities and imperatives. An extract from the risk management policy for NHS Direct is included as a case study at the end of Part IV; see pp 177–178.

The risk management manual will include all of the static risk management documentation. Although smaller organizations may not produce a formalized risk management manual, the features described in the manual will, nevertheless, need to be established for any organization that takes a formalized approach to the management of risk. Depending on the size, nature and complexity of an organization, the risk management manual could be a comprehensive document containing at least the following sections:

- risk management strategy statement that sets out the risk agenda for the organization, including the objectives of the risk management initiative, and business rationale for managing risk;

- roles and responsibilities for risk management, including those of individuals and the terms of reference and reporting lines of committees with risk management responsibilities;
- details of protocols and procedures within the organization related to risk management, covering all five components of the risk management cube shown as Figure I in the Introduction; and
- details of the risk management documentation that is required, including the static (or reference) documents, as well as the dynamic documents that drive and monitor risk management actions, such as the risk action plan.

The risk management strategy statement is sometimes referred to as the 'risk management policy' and it is normally issued as a one-page statement outlining the risk agenda. Overall, the risk management manual enables an organization to establish detailed procedures on a range of risk management topics, as well as setting out the risk management priorities for the following year. For example, many organizations produce an annual health and safety and/or environmental policy and this should be an integral part of the risk management manual. The following box provides an overview of the contents of a simple risk management manual.

Contents of a risk management manual

Aim of this document

The aim of this risk management manual is to detail the corporate risk management policy and procedures. It should be read by executive team members and their direct reports who in turn should explain the policy and procedures to their staff.

Contents

1 Statement of the risk management strategy
2 Completion of the corporate risk register
3 Roles and responsibilities for risk
4 Risk protocols and procedures
    Annex A: Risk probability/impact setting
    Annex B: Aid to identifying risks
    Annex C: Risk register template

Each type of risk management documentation, as discussed in Chapter 13, may result in several individual documents being prepared by an organization. For example, specific risk statements may be legal requirements. A health and safety policy statement is a specific example. Details of the standards that should be achieved may be included in these specific risk management policy statements. Various risk protocols and procedures will need to be established, together with associated records of awareness training.

In this book, the rules, procedures and guidelines describing how risk management activity shall be undertaken are referred to as the 'risk protocols'. The protocols for risk management will need to be established for all organizations. In many cases, these will be established in writing, but this may not be necessary for small and medium-sized enterprises. The risk protocols will often include details of the (internal) control responsibilities of managers.

Risk roles and responsibilities

Figure 14.1 illustrates the committee structure that could exist within a medium-sized organization. The purpose of Figure 14.1 is to focus on the risk and risk management components of the committee structure, often referred to as the 'risk architecture' for the organization. The committee structure is headed by the board and this will typically have executive and non-executive directors. In relation to risk management responsibilities, the board will focus on two broad issues: 1) setting the strategy for the organization and monitoring progress with the implementation of that strategy; and 2) governance of the organization, including specific consideration of risk and risk management.

In a typical medium-sized or large company, the day-to-day management of the organization will be the responsibility of the executive committee, which will normally include the executive members of the board, together with the other members of the senior management team, often referred to collectively as 'top management'. The executive committee will be responsible for a wide range of issues, but all of them are associated with the success of the organization.

To illustrate the risk architecture, Figure 14.1 defines the main risk and risk management responsibilities of key committees. These committees are illustrated as the operations committee and commercial

FIGURE 14.1 Typical risk architecture

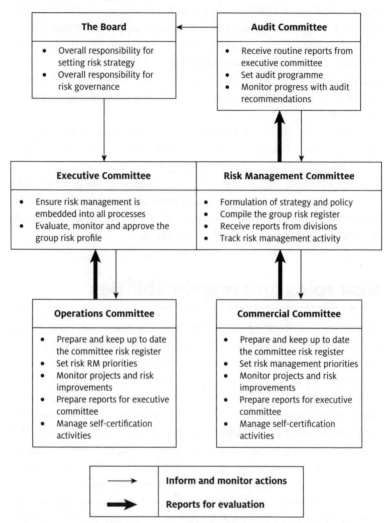

committee. The operations committee has responsibility for the internal finances and the infrastructure of the organization. The commercial committee has responsibility for the external reputation and marketplace success of the organization. In each case, the risk management responsibilities of the committees are defined in the same way.

The risk architecture represented in Figure 14.1 will be supplemented by details of the terms of reference of the various committees. The terms will include details of the membership and responsibilities of the various committees. The risk architecture should also indicate how risk information is communicated between the various committees. Figure 14.1 shows the executive committee and risk committee side-by-side. Depending on the size, nature and complexity of the organization, these committees may be separate.

Alternatively, the organization may decide that a separate risk committee is not required and the executive committee will have responsibility for the issues that would otherwise have been allocated to the separate risk committee. The details of the agenda, frequency of meetings and membership of the individual committees will need to be decided by the organization and defined by the terms of reference of the committees.

Clear definition of risk management roles and responsibilities is essential in all organizations. The extent to which this information is consolidated into a written risk management manual will vary. The importance of the risk management manual is discussed later in this chapter; it is important that the manual fully reflects the risk agenda for the organization.

Risk management and committees

The decision on whether to have a separate risk committee and where it should fit into the risk architecture will depend on the size, nature and complexity of the organization. Many highly regulated organizations will establish a separate risk committee to oversee risk and risk management; having separate risk committees in financial institutions has become fairly standard practice. The terms of reference of a separate risk committee in a financial institution would probably identify the primary role of that committee as overseeing compliance with the requirements of Basel II in the case of a bank, or Solvency II in the case of an insurance company based in Europe.

Terms of reference of the risk committee

The following is an edited extract of information that appears on the Network Rail website:

The main responsibilities of the audit and risk committee are to monitor the integrity of the financial reporting and the audit process and to monitor internal control systems including risk management, regulation and compliance. The committee makes recommendations to the board on the level of risk appetite acceptable to the company and oversees the process for the identification and management of risk. The committee has a structured programme of activities including receipt of regular detailed reports on relevant aspects of management, focused to coincide with key events of the annual financial reporting cycle.

As the risk committee in a financial institution is primarily concerned with compliance issues, it is likely that it will have a membership of non-executive directors and report to the audit committee. Indeed, for all organizations that are taking a passive approach to risk management, a separate risk committee reporting to the audit committee may be appropriate. The primary purpose of the risk committee in these circumstances will be to provide assurance of compliance with risk management obligations. Some organizations have a combined risk and audit committee, as described by Network Rail in the box.

For organizations that wish to take a proactive approach, the management of risk becomes more clearly an executive function. In these circumstances, it is likely that an executive committee will be allocated responsibility for risk management. Figure 14.1 illustrates a typical arrangement in organizations taking a proactive approach to risk management. The figure shows risk management as an executive function. It also represents circumstances where the risk committee may be a separate committee, as well as circumstances where risk management may simply be one of the responsibilities of the executive committee.

Regardless of the motivation for undertaking risk management, the terms of reference and membership of the committee responsible for risk need to be carefully established. If the motivation is primarily compliance, a non-executive committee with the additional attendance of executive directors, external auditors and risk management specialists will be appropriate. This will provide an attendance list very similar to that of the audit committee.

For smaller companies, development of formalized risk architecture may be disproportionate. Nevertheless, one of the key features of Figure 14.1 is the illustration of the roles and responsibilities that need to be allocated within an organization. In smaller organizations, these responsibilities will (perhaps informally in some cases) be allocated to individuals rather than committees. The key principles for risk management, as described in Chapter 3, are that activities associated with risk and risk management should be proportionate, aligned and dynamic, and responsibilities need to be allocated to ensure that these principles are achieved.

A relevant consideration for organizations setting up a risk committee is to decide whether the committee will be a head office directing and monitoring function or an across the company committee that also shares experiences. If the committee is primarily concerned with compliance, it is likely to be a senior level committee with director membership only, together with attendance of specialists. If the committee is also a learning committee, a broader attendance from across the organization will be required. In either case, the main risk committee may be supported by specialist learning sub-committees, such as health and safety.

Developing risk protocols

A wide range of risk protocols and procedures may be required, even in a small organization. The organization will decide the extent to which these will be recorded in writing. In broad terms, the organization should evaluate the need for established protocols in relation to at least the following:

- risk assessment procedures, including details of when risk assessments should be carried out, how the output from the assessments should be recorded and how risk improvement recommendations are monitored;
- risk control objectives, including setting standards in relation to specific types of risks such as health and safety, environmental

protection, contract risk and expectations of the insurance programme;

- risk resourcing arrangements, including details of required in-house expertise, requirements for external specialist advice and arrangements for internal and external audit;
- resilience planning requirements, including details of disaster recovery and business continuity plans, as well as reference to 'after the risk event' cost containment requirements; and
- risk assurance reports, including information on maintenance of the risk register, terms of reference of relevant committees and details of self-certification arrangements.

When developing risk protocols, the organization should decide the protocols and procedures that are relevant to strategy, tactics, operations and compliance. It should decide the risk management input that is required into strategy development and implementation. Also, the need for a risk assessment to be attached to capital expenditure and other investment projects should be specified in the risk protocols. The requirements of risk protocols should ensure that risk management activities are aligned with other activities in the organization.

Risk management activities within the organization should be aligned with the other business operations, processes and imperatives. For example, many organizations will already have authorization limits and some larger organizations will consolidate financial control procedures into a document that is often called a 'delegation of authority'. If such a document already exists, it should be recognized as a document containing risk protocols.

The risk protocols should define the means by which embedded risk management is to be achieved in the organization. The setting of strategy, standards and procedures needs to be undertaken within the framework of the risk protocols. The format for the risk protocols will depend on the organization and the nature of the risks that it faces. Typically, these guidelines will contain information on at least the following:

- financial and authorization procedures;
- insurance arrangements;
- managers' control responsibilities;
- project risk management;
- incident reporting and investigation;

- event and reaction planning;
- physical risk control objectives and responsibilities;
- risk escalation requirements and arrangements;
- communication arrangements for whistleblowing.

There should be a relationship between the risk management manual, the risk architecture and the risk protocols in the organization. The risk management manual will collect together all procedures associated with risk management, although in a smaller organization this may be part of a policies and procedures manual. It is worth remembering that the risk management manual is the collection of static documents for the organization. The dynamic documents that record the risk action plan, records of risk training, reports of risk events and routine monitoring reports of risk performance will also be kept. In many cases, these dynamic documents will be the results of following the protocols set out in the risk management manual.

Other documentation is relevant to the risk management manual, including delegation of authority documents, authorization procedures and limits. Also, the risk management manual should set out information on the benchmarks that have been established to define when a risk is significant to the organization. Capital expenditure procedures and requirements for a risk assessment to be attached to strategy documents that are presented to the executive committee or the board should also be specified.

In summary, the risk protocols should be proportionate, aligned with other activities in the organization and dynamic to changing circumstances. The case study of Organate Foods described in Appendix 1 provides a practical example of the range of risk protocols that need to be developed for a small organization. One of the case studies at the end of this part of the book is the risk management policy for NHS Direct (see pp 177–178); this reinforces the need to embed risk management within day-to-day activities.

CHAPTER FIFTEEN

RISK ACTION PLAN

Designing a suitable risk register

The purpose of the risk register is to create an agreed record of the significant risks that have been identified. Also, the risk register will serve as a record of the control activities that are currently undertaken. It may also serve as a record of the additional actions that are proposed to improve the control of a particular risk. To be an effective and complete record of the output from the risk assessment workshop, the risk register should include the information required about each risk, as described in Chapter 1.

The use of risk registers has become established practice for many risk management practitioners, when recording the output from a risk assessment workshop that has considered the risks to the infrastructure of the organization. There are difficulties associated with the use of risk registers, including the danger that the information recorded will not be used in a dynamic way to improve risk management performance. The risk register could become a static record of risk status, rather than act as the risk action plan for the organization.

Risk registers can be compiled in a number of formats, depending on the type of risk assessment being recorded. The design of the risk register will need to be appropriate for the organization itself and the feature of the organization that is the subject of the risk assessment. If risk assessment is undertaken for passive reasons, it may well be a list of risks and a statement of controls that, taken together, provide assurance that appropriate risk management activities are taking place within the organization. This becomes a risk governance report, rather than a risk action plan.

By way of an example of what would be recorded in a risk register, the list below shows the risks that may be identified by a professional football club when it undertakes a risk assessment of the whole organization. At this stage, the list of risks is presented as those events with the potential to have a significant negative impact on the finances, infrastructure, reputation and marketplace activities of the club:

- Financial risks, including insufficient funds available for the purchase of new players and the pension fund reserves being inadequate to meet liabilities.
- Infrastructure risks, including the loss of a highly respected young manager and the building of the new stadium being delayed.
- Reputational risks, including complaints that merchandise is too expensive and the unruly behaviour of club supporters at away games.
- Marketplace risks, including comments that attendance at recent games has decreased and the new range of merchandise is unattractive.

This list represents the significant risks to the club with the potential to impact above the benchmark test for significance. This list can form the basis of the risk register for the club, although more information will be required on the controls that are in place. The list of risks, together with the additional controls information, can also form the basis on which assurances can be given to the board, audit committee and club financiers that appropriate attention is paid to risk management throughout the organization.

Having undertaken this risk assessment exercise, the club will then need to evaluate these risks in terms of the anticipated consequences for strategy, tactics, operations and compliance. Taking the list of risks in the risk register and converting that list into a set of actions beneficial to the organization will convert the risk register from a risk assurance document to a proactive risk action plan. This conversion represents a challenge to the club management to take the output from the risk assessment and convert it into a set of actions that will provide beneficial outcomes for the organization.

At its most simple, the risk register can be stored on a computer. However, there are many more sophisticated forms of risk registers, including records of significant risks held on databases. Where quantification of exposure is required, a simple risk register held as a document is unlikely to be sufficient. Financial institutions are required to undertake the quantification of operational risk exposure and the recording of this information requires sophisticated software packages. The quantification of risk exposures is undertaken by financial institutions in response to mandatory requirements, such as Basel II for banks and Solvency II for insurance companies operating in Europe.

When a risk assessment of strategic options or a risk assessment of an investment decision is undertaken, it is more usual for the risk assessment to be used as part of the decision-making process. Typically, the result of the risk assessment will not be recorded in the format of a risk register, but will be presented to the decision maker as part of the full range of information available for making that strategic decision. However, it should be noted that as this information is presented to support decision making, it represents a passive approach to the management of risk. When risk information is used for proactive reasons, it is better if the information is embedded in existing management information streams and actively used as part of the day-to-day management of the organization.

Risk register and risk action plan

Despite the potential dangers, a well-constructed and dynamic risk register is at the heart of a successful risk management initiative. However, the organization will have to ensure that senior management does not believe that attending a risk assessment workshop and producing a risk register fulfil their risk management obligations and no ongoing actions are required. Even when risk management activities are undertaken for passive reasons, the organization has to be aware of changing circumstances and emerging risks. Therefore, it is unlikely that any organization will be able to undertake risk management activities for entirely passive reasons.

When risk management is specifically undertaken for more proactive reasons, the risk register may not be the most appropriate means of recording risk information. It is often the case that the additional actions that are required are recorded in a risk register in a way that does not clearly identify precisely what should be done, who should do it and the deadline for completing the actions. Even if the risk register is intended to act as a risk action plan, the way in which information is recorded may often make auditing of further actions difficult.

When further control actions are identified as being necessary, the organization should extract information from the risk register and prepare a more detailed and comprehensive risk action plan. In any case, if the organization is specifically seeking a more dynamic output from the risk assessment exercise and is undertaking risk management for proactive reasons, the preparation of a risk action plan is essential. Above all, the additional actions described in a risk action plan need to be auditable, in terms of the actions being taken and the effectiveness and efficiency of the enhanced controls that are being introduced.

Designing a suitable risk action plan

Part of the analysis that is required when developing the risk action plan is to consider the opportunities for implementing cost-effective risk improvements. Some organizations have produced grades defining risk improvement opportunities to assist with the identification of risk improvement priorities. The following is an edited extract from the University of Aberdeen website:

Ability to manage grid:

1 *Unmanageable external risk – (essentially) no ability to influence the risk or its consequences, such as introduction of new general legislation.*

2 *External risk with limited ability to manage – only limited ability to influence the risk or its consequences, such as introduction of changes to fire service at national level.*

3 *External risk with significant ability to manage – can influence the impact and/or likelihood of occurrence, such as arson, computer hacking.*

4 *Internal risk that is not fully manageable – can largely influence the impact and/or likelihood of occurrence, such as staff retention, machinery breakdown.*

5 *Internal risk that is essentially fully manageable – can wholly influence the impact and/or likelihood of occurrence, such as overspend/delay on project execution.*

The involvement of risk management in the successful delivery of projects is now well established. For example, a significant risk management capability was developed within the Olympic Delivery Authority to ensure the success of the London Games in 2012. The main feature of successful project risk management is that the project risk register becomes a very dynamic document. The details of the risks to the project are discussed at every project review meeting and actions are debated and agreed so that the project cost/delivery/quality remains on schedule.

Risk communication protocols

Part of the risk assessment process should be to determine the means by which risk information will be communicated. The risk register or risk action plan contains the vitally important summary information on the risk status of the organization. Sharing the risk register with the board, audit committee and other relevant stakeholders is part of a robust risk communication protocol. However, this also involves communicating with staff, managers and top management to ensure that they all understand their roles and responsibilities. The GSK case study at the end of this part of the book (see p 180) confirms the importance of risk communication with shareholders.

Risk communication

The importance of risk communication is recognized by many organizations and the following is an edited extract from the website of Thames Water:

> It is vital that we communicate our plans and progress on our wide variety of network and site improvement projects which are likely to affect residents, businesses and other members of our community. Communication activities include organizing 'drop-in' sessions for local people to meet project representatives; producing letters and leaflets explaining our work; gathering customer feedback on our activities; organizing site tours, home visits for personal engagement and initiating or taking part in community outreach to build local relationships. Communications are carried out in collaboration with the contractors who carry out improvements on our behalf.

One of the main reasons for communicating risk information and providing risk training is to ensure that a consistent response to similar risk events is always achieved. This can only be ensured by sharing information and experience in relation to all types of risks. The organization's intranet is an ideal way of achieving a consistent response to risk by ensuring that appropriate information is always readily available.

Risk protocols also need to be defined and communicated. Part of ensuring a consistent response to risk is to identify risks in advance and confirm the controls that have been put in place for them. An important consideration related to the need for consistent responses to risk is when a new risk appears or an existing risk changes substantially. In these circumstances, risk escalation may be required so that the changed conditions are brought to the attention of senior management. The design and introduction of robust risk escalation procedures is required, with appropriate training provided in these procedures.

When a disaster recovery plan has been produced, training for directors, managers and staff is essential. Also, the requirements of the business continuity plan will need to be communicated to all those who may be affected if the plan is implemented. Again, the importance of training to ensure a consistent response to adverse circumstances is essential. (Disaster recovery and business continuity planning were discussed in more detail in Chapter 11.)

Improving the arrangements for risk communication in any organization will increase awareness of risks and should result in improved risk performance. Enhanced risk communication with external stakeholders will improve the reputation of the organization, as well as increasing confidence with stakeholders, especially shareholders. Likewise, open risk communication will result in an improved relationship with regulators.

Risk culture and risk maturity

Risk culture and risk maturity are important concepts that are relevant to the success of risk management within organizations. An increasingly risk-aware culture, together with an advanced level of risk maturity and risk sophistication will result in enhanced levels of risk management. In turn, this should bring a better understanding of the risks faced by the organization, both in terms of potential impact and anticipated consequences.

There have been many attempts to define risk culture and risk maturity, often in somewhat academic papers. Nevertheless, all organizations will recognize that risk awareness within the organization is a beneficial characteristic that should result in increased success. (Chapter 4 considered the attributes of an organization that has achieved a high level of embedded risk management.)

Although there are formalized models to measure risk culture, an empirical approach that considers the components of achieving embedded risk management is equally valid. It is now generally accepted that the following attributes are present in an organization that has achieved embedded risk management and developed a good risk-aware culture:

- *Leadership* – strong leadership within the organization in relation to strategy, projects, operations and compliance.
- *Involvement* – involvement of all stakeholders in all stages of the risk management strategy and protocols.
- *Learning* – emphasis on training in risk management procedures and learning from risk events.
- *Accountability* – absence of an automatic blame culture, but appropriate accountability for actions.
- *Communication* – communication and openness on all risk management issues and the lessons learnt.

The actions that should be taken to increase risk awareness

The management of a transport company has decided that a campaign to increase the risk awareness of drivers is required. It has been decided that this campaign will focus mainly on road traffic accidents, as well as correct and timely delivery. The overall objective is to achieve a risk-aware culture that makes drivers aware of the risks and the relevant controls, as well as encouraging them to contribute to the reduction in total risk exposure of the company.

It has been recognized that a campaign that just uses one means of communication will be unsuccessful. Therefore, the company has decided to launch an awareness campaign that will include:

- allocation of responsibilities;
- risk awareness training;

- awareness poster campaigns;
- site inspections;
- arrangements for reporting defects;
- leaflets and brochures;
- a risk reporting helpline;
- liaison with the local police.

As the risk awareness in an organization increases, the organization is likely to become more sophisticated in its approach to risk management. At first, it may recognize that it needs to reform its protocols to comply with risk management requirements. Having achieved conformity, the organization should then be able to move to a position where risk management helps with improved efficiency and effectiveness of strategy, tactics, operations and compliance.

However, there is a danger that if the organization becomes obsessed with risk, there will be an over-dependence on risk management processes. This may not be as much of a problem for organizations that are undertaking risk management for passive reasons, but will be a real obstacle for those seeking to take a more proactive approach. In other words, the increasingly diligent production of lists of risks that are recorded in a risk register may actually serve to inhibit innovation and success within the organization.

CHAPTER SIXTEEN

RISK REPORTING

Internal risk communication

The scope of activities covered by internal risk communication within an organization will be far-reaching. Internal risk communication includes information that is informally provided to staff by way of training and instruction. Communication is relevant to the entire contents of the risk management manual, disaster recovery and business continuity plans, as well as the more formal means of communication, such as the results of a risk assessment exercise and reports of risk events that have occurred. (The contents of the risk management manual were considered in Chapter 14.)

The design and use of the risk register and risk action plan were considered in Chapter 15. It is likely to be the case for most organizations that the most important documents concerned with internal risk communication will be the risk register and/or the risk action plan. These documents will contain information on the significant risks faced by the organization and they will be critically important documents, regardless of whether the organization undertakes risk management activities for passive or proactive reasons.

The importance of the risk register should be acknowledged within the organization and it should be designed and used to communicate risk information effectively. In many cases, the risk register will be the basis of providing assurance to stakeholders on the risk management activities within the organization. The risk register will contain details of the significant risks faced by the organization, together with information on emerging risks. However, the fact that some of this information may be confidential should be recognized within the communication procedures.

Risk communication activities should be designed to ensure that the key stakeholders are aware of the risks faced by the organization and their role and responsibilities in the management of those risks. The range of risk communication activities undertaken should align with the risk agenda that has been established. The overall purpose of risk communication is to ensure that the appropriate level of risk awareness exists within the organization and a consistent response to risk is always achieved.

It is important for the organization to establish the risk architecture, strategy and protocols for the management of risk information. Details of the risk architecture and protocols will be set out in the risk management manual. The risk architecture should be designed so that it can deliver the risk communication requirements of the organization. For example, internal lagging indicators providing information on risk performance are an important part of risk communication and the means by which this information is shared should be confirmed. Also, the risk architecture should make provision for whistleblowing arrangements.

The case study set out in Appendix 1 provides information on the internal risk communication arrangements within Organate Foods. As with all risk management activities, the arrangements for internal risk communication should be proportionate to the size, nature and complexity of the organization and the level of risk that it faces. Aligning internal risk management communication with other activities in the organization will ensure that necessary information regarding risk exposure is available to the relevant people at the appropriate time. The importance of risk communication is demonstrated by the example set out in the following box.

Importance of risk communication

Awareness of the level of risk within an organization is vitally important. Sometimes, the information needs to be updated on an almost continuous basis. For a police authority, it may be appropriate to have a daily briefing of police officers on the current status of police activities in their area, as follows:

Each morning our operations team receive briefings from each of the local police areas, highlighting incidents in the previous 24 hours.

> *The ability to ensure resilience at all times requires monitoring of exceptional incidents and the sharing of intelligence or information about planned police activity. A daily briefing meeting takes place for the senior officer in operational command of the force that day.*

Many organizations will communicate risk information internally by means of a shared database, or on the intranet. The intranet is a useful way of ensuring that the risk information is always accessible and up to date. A wide range of risk information can be available on the company intranet, including the provision of training materials. Internal electronic communications can also be used to obtain risk information from different departments within the organization, as well as notification of incidents and/or losses.

External risk reporting

In addition to internal risk communication, external risk communication will also be required. Often, this external risk communication is related to mandatory risk reporting requirements. All types of organizations are required to undertake risk management activities, including central and local government, health services, emergency services, charities and public listed companies. Even if the organization does not fit into any of these categories, it is probable that external stakeholders will require the reporting of risk information, the most likely of which will be regulators and financiers.

Although the exact requirements vary, most stock exchanges around the world require organizations to undertake risk management. Some listing authorities require a description of the organization's risk agenda, together with the risk management activities that take place. This is not always necessary, but it has become fairly standard for organizations to be required to list and describe the risk factors they face. Although it is not always a specific disclosure requirement, it is the description of the risk architecture and protocols that provides the greater insight into the arrangements for managing risks in the organization.

Importance of risk reporting

Many organizations recognize the value of good risk reporting; set out below is an edited extract from the website of Solvay SA:

Besides overall good management, control practices and systems, efficient communication (transparent, consistent and timely) and long-term solid relationships, both inside and outside the organization, contribute in the long run to establishing trust, which is a fundamental ingredient to reputation. In addition to fostering its own good reputation, Solvay participates in specific programmes implemented by key trade organizations to improve the reputation of the entire chemical industry.

A study of Solvay's enterprise risk management maturity mentioned reputational management as one of Solvay's risk management strengths. Solvay has established communication processes, systems, plans and programmes to create, develop and maintain a regular flow of two-way communication with the main stakeholders: shareholders and the financial community, employees, customers, authorities, local communities and opinion leaders.

Tools include a variety of internal and external electronic and print media tailored for internal and external audiences. Solvay maintains active press relations at corporate and local level, with press releases, conferences and visits as well as open doors and other events aimed at local residents around major sites.

Charities are offered tax and other benefits in most countries, and will seek to achieve those benefits by being registered with the regulator. It is typical for the regulator to require that risk management activities take place within the registered charities. Reporting on those activities becomes a mandatory requirement of maintaining registration and continuing to gain the benefits that are associated with charitable status.

Although most types of organizations are required to undertake risk management activities, the scope of the activities is usually restricted to assurance that all significant risks have been identified and controlled. Assurance has to be provided by all of these agencies to the relevant regulators and/or government audit bodies. In addition, many organizations need to report their risk management activities to other stakeholders. It will be more persuasive if the organization can explain that it undertakes proactive risk management, whereby the anticipated consequences of risks occurring are being actively managed.

One of the biggest steps forward in external risk reporting in recent times has been the willingness of governments to be more open about security threats. For example, the UK government has published the National Risk Register. This is an example of government itself recognizing the importance of external risk reporting and ensuring that as much information as possible is put in the public domain, consistent with the need to protect national security. The risks that were considered most significant for the UK government are set out in the following box.

National government security assessment

Within this analysis, there is no mention of the objectives or key dependencies of the UK or the UK government. However, the threat analysis is robust and detailed. The threat categories to UK national security identified in the document include the following:

- natural events, including weather, coastal and river flooding and pandemic human or animal disease;
- major incidents, including terrorist attack on infrastructure and major industrial or transport accidents; and
- malicious attacks on crowded places, transport and electronic infrastructure (including nuclear or nonconventional attack).

Completing statutory risk reports

Many organizations are required to submit risk reports as a consequence of being listed on a stock exchange. Sometimes, the organization will take the approach of reporting the minimum information that is required. On other occasions, a more expansive approach is taken and information beyond the statutory minimum is supplied. The case study at the end of this part of the book relates to information in the GSK Annual Report 2011 (see p 180). This information indicates that GSK liaises with shareholders in a formal and structured way that is beyond statutory risk reporting requirements.

Many listed companies report the risk factors relevant to their range of activities. This is useful information and is intended to supply shareholders (and other stakeholders) with information about the risks to the company. The primary reason for providing this information is to enable potential shareholders to identify the level of risk associated with holding that stock. Some listed companies go beyond the minimum statutory requirements and provide insight into their broader risk agenda. For other organizations, however, the level of information provided is little more than what is obvious given the size of the organization and the sector in which it operates.

At the end of this part of the book, and also at the end of Parts I, II, III and V, there are extracts from the report and accounts of listed companies. These examples illustrate good practice in risk reporting and provide further insight into the risk agendas for the companies. When a listed company provides information beyond the minimum statutory requirements, greater assurance is provided, because shareholders can evaluate the risk management protocols and procedures in place.

As well as requirements related to risk reporting for listed companies, attention to risk management in government departments and other areas of the public sector is usually mandatory. Much of the information on risk management in government bodies is freely available on websites and is very useful reference material. Several of the examples used in this book have been obtained from the websites of police, ambulance, university and other public authorities. Although police authorities place a good deal of risk information in the public domain, information will not be provided where it could undermine police operations.

Risk reporting by charities is compulsory in most countries. The range of risks faced by charities can be challenging and will relate to the way in which funds are raised and the risks associated with fulfilling the purpose of the charity. Accordingly, charities need to pay considerable attention to the governance of fundraising activities and, having accounted for all money that has been raised, the charity then faces perhaps an even greater challenge of ensuring that funds that have been raised go towards its charitable objectives.

For many charities, risk management will be undertaken on a passive basis in relation to the control of funds and fundraising. However, if the operations of the charity present risks to staff and volunteers, risk management activities will have a much more proactive focus. The study of charities and the ways in which they manage risk can provide many examples of good risk management practice. The case study on Oxfam at the end of Part I (see pp oo) provides an insight into the risk agenda of that charity.

What should be in the risk report to the UK Charity Commission?

A report to the UK Charity Commission may include the following:

- risk assessment processes are in place to identify priority significant risks facing the strategy of the charity;
- risk management policies, processes and procedures are embedded into routine operations;
- procedures are in place to ensure legal compliance, including routine reports on legal matters to the board of trustees;
- training provided for trustees on risk management and corporate governance issues relevant to the charity;
- reports that are received by trustees of risk management activities and evaluation of the control environment;
- additional reports about any significant weaknesses in controls and details of any material failures of controls.

PART IV REVIEW

Checklist

The checklist for risk communication provides four items that should be reviewed to confirm that appropriate risk communication activities have been developed and implemented for the organization. The starting point for developing an appropriate approach to risk communication is to complete a riskiness index described in Chapter 1 and analyse the extent to which risk events could have a potential impact on finances, infrastructure, reputation or marketplace.

The overall objective of internal risk communication activities is to ensure that risk information is shared throughout the organization. This will support good decision making and ensure that a consistent response to risk is achieved. External risk reporting is usually concerned with providing stakeholders with risk assurance. Risk assurance will also ensure that the company is able to confirm that the significant risks to the organization have been identified and managed to the appropriate level.

Organizations should also take a proactive approach to risk management to improve the efficiency and effectiveness of strategy, tactics, operations and compliance. If the organization is successfully going to achieve proactive management of risk, then risk communication becomes even more important. It is especially important that information about risks is shared and feedback and/or additional comment from the recipient of the information are encouraged.

The checklist below is intended to focus on the priority risk communication activities for an organization when it is designing and implementing a comprehensive risk management initiative. It sets out the issues relevant to risk communication that need to be clarified by the organization.

---

1. Describe the risk architecture and protocols for the organization, including the risk management roles and responsibilities of individuals; the terms of reference for committees with risk management responsibilities; and the risk management policies and procedures.

2. Describe the risk management documentation that should be kept by the organization, including information on risk communication arrangements and the requirements for risk management training, and determine the level to which a written risk management manual is required.

3. Determine the means for recording the results of the risk assessments in the organization, including relevant information about the significant risks and the level to which assurance can be provided regarding the acceptable or tolerable level of risk, and design a suitable risk register.

4. Plan the risk reporting arrangements, including details of progress with risk action plans, risk improvement initiatives and risk reduction programmes, as well as details of risk escalation procedures, external risk reporting procedures and, as necessary, whistleblowing arrangements.

Case studies

NHS Direct: risk management policy

Introduction

NHS Direct is committed to minimizing risk through a framework of integrated governance supported by a proactive risk management culture. In accordance with our agreed clinical assumptions, we will prioritize patient safety, taking account of risks and benefits to the patient. This policy addresses the service needs of NHS Direct and the requirements for an effective system of internal control in line with guidance from the Department of Health.

Purpose

To establish and communicate the policy of NHS Direct regarding corporate risk management and to describe key roles and responsibilities of individuals involved in the process of risk management. This policy covers everyone that is employed by NHS Direct and any contractors and partners.

Policy statement

It is the policy of NHS Direct that:

- Risk management shall be an integral part of day-to-day management and quality improvement at all levels within the Trust. NHS Direct shall adopt a whole systems approach encompassing risks in relation to integrated governance. In accordance with our clinical assumptions, in taking decisions about the management of risk, we will prioritize patient safety.
- Risk management shall be as much about identifying opportunities to succeed as avoiding failure and mitigating losses.
- A robust risk management process and effective ongoing communications will assist in safeguarding the reputation and assets from litigation and adverse media interest. Risk management systems will comply with all relevant statutory and regulatory requirements.

- Key performance indicators for risk management shall be developed, implemented and reviewed to measure the effectiveness of the risk management system.
- An integrated approach to risk management shall be adopted where risks are aligned to business objectives at all levels of the organization.
- Risk management processes at all levels of the organization will be aligned.
- Acceptable levels of risk shall be determined by the external circumstances, together with the risk appetite of the board and its key stakeholders.
- The board shall approve a means of determining the way in which risks are scored in terms of likelihood and consequence.

Roles and responsibilities

All staff and managers have responsibility for risk management and specific roles have been allocated. The key risk management roles and responsibilities are differentiated from functional roles and advisory/compliance roles and are consistent with the different levels of risk reporting that exist.

(Based on information on the NHS Direct website 2012.)

Morrisons: risk and uncertainties

Risk is accepted as being a part of doing business and within the group responsibility for risk management and internal control lies with the board. Through the application of reasoned judgement and consideration of the likelihood and consequence of events, the board believes a successful risk management framework balances risk and reward. The list below sets out some of the most significant risks to the achievement of group business goals.

Business strategy

In the long term, effectively managing the strategic risks that the group faces will deliver benefits to all our stakeholders. To ensure that our strategy is communicated and understood, the group engages with a wide range of stakeholders including shareholders, employees, suppliers and other groups. The board is conscious of the difficult economic environment in which it operates, with rising unemployment, reduced spending power and high levels of anxiety amongst customers.

Product quality and safety

We recognize that the quality and safety of our products is of critical importance to us and that any failure in this regard would affect the confidence of our customers in us. We work with our suppliers to ensure the integrity of the products supplied. Also, as a manufacturer of food products, we maintain strict standards and monitoring processes to manage the risks associated with food safety throughout our group and its supply chain. Food hygiene practices are taken very seriously throughout our group, and are monitored both through internal audit procedures and external bodies. We have well-prepared procedures for crisis management in order to act quickly when required.

Corporate social responsibility

In line with our commercial objectives we have identified three areas: environment, society and business where, by 'doing the right thing', we protect valuable resources, meet demand for sustainable products and make our business more efficient. Morrisons is committed to taking good care of our environment and if we fail to meet our commitments this could damage our reputation and possibly lose the trust of our stakeholders.

Business interruption

Our distribution and systems infrastructures are fundamental to ensuring the normal continuity of trading in our stores. If a major incident occurred to this infrastructure or another key facility, this would have a detrimental impact on the business's ability to operate effectively. The current challenging economic environment increases the risk that one of our key suppliers is adversely impacted by the recession and is unable to supply our stores. We mitigate the potential impact of this on our business by seeking several sources of supply for products wherever possible.

(Edited extract from Morrisons Annual Report and Accounts 2009.)

GSK: relations with shareholders

We work to engage effectively with shareholders through our regular communications, the AGM and other investor relations activities. We announce our financial results on a quarterly basis. The annual results are included in our annual report. All shareholders receive an annual summary leaflet which advises them that our annual report and notice of our annual general meeting are available on our website.

Our CEO and CFO give live presentations to institutional investors, analysts and media with the half and full year results, which are also available via webcast and teleconference. After the first and third quarter results, we hold webcast teleconferences for the same audience. Our results are available on our website.

Our investor relations department, with offices in London and Philadelphia, acts as a focal point for communications with investors. The CEO, CFO and chairman maintain a continuous dialogue with institutional shareholders on performance, plans and objectives through a programme of regular meetings. During the year, over 240 meetings were held with major shareholders.

The company secretary acts as a focal point for communications on corporate governance matters. We also have a small central corporate responsibility team which coordinates strategy, policy development and reporting specifically with respect to corporate responsibility and communicates with socially responsible investors and other stakeholders.

The chairman also meets regularly with institutional shareholders to hear their views and discuss issues of mutual importance and communicates their views to the other members of the board. The senior independent director and all the non-executive directors are available to meet with shareholders.

The chairman of remuneration, the chairman, the head of human resources and the company secretary hold annual meetings with major shareholders to discuss executive remuneration and governance matters. We have a briefing process in place, managed by the chairman, for non-executive directors to focus on sector-specific issues and general shareholder preferences.

(Edited extract from GSK Annual Report 2011.)

Further reading

BSI (2011) *British Standard BS 31100 (2011): Risk Management. Code of practice and guidance for the implementation of BS ISO 31000*, www.standardsuk.com

COSO (2004) *Enterprise Risk Management – Integrated framework, executive summary*, www.coso.org

Financial Reporting Council (2005) *Internal Control. Revised guidance for directors on the Combined Code*, www.frc.org.uk.

HM Treasury (2004) *Orange Book, Management of risk – principles and concepts*, www.hm-treasury.gov.uk

Hopkin, P (2012) *Fundamentals of Risk Management*, ISBN 978-0-7494-6539-1, Kogan Page: www.koganpage.com

Institute of Chartered Accountants in England and Wales (2002) *Risk Management for SMEs*, www.icaew.com

Institute of Risk Management (2002) *A Risk Management Standard*, www.theirm.org

Institute of Risk Management (2010) *Structured Approach to Enterprise Risk Management and the Requirements of ISO 31000*, www.theirm.org

Part V
Risk
governance

This component requires the organization to consider the risk management expectations of stakeholders and the provision of risk assurance, as well as introduce appropriate governance procedures for existing and emerging risks.

Importance of risk governance

Part V is concerned with risk governance and the sources of assurance available for internal and external stakeholders. The risk governance component defines how the organization is going to design and implement suitable arrangements to provide assurance to key stakeholders and establish procedures for governance of existing and emerging risks.

The extent of risk governance activities will depend on the size, nature and complexity of the organization and the requirements of external stakeholders, especially financiers and regulators. Key features in the development of risk governance procedures include identification of key stakeholders, their risk management expectations and the means by which they will be provided with risk assurance, including formal and informal reporting arrangements; and design and implementation of suitable and sufficient governance procedures for the management of known or existing risks and, especially, developing and emerging risks.

Assurance is a very important concept in the successful management of risk. If the organization undertakes risk management activities for passive reasons, providing risk assurance becomes one of the primary motivations. If risk management is undertaken because it is mandatory, the organization will need to provide assurance to the regulator, financier or client that adequate risk management activities are being carried out.

There is a close link between the provision of assurance and the expectations of stakeholders in relation to risk management activities. All organizations will have a wide range of stakeholders, as discussed in more detail in Chapter 20. Stakeholders will include customers, staff, financiers, suppliers, regulators and society. Each will have different risk management expectations, but all will require assurance regarding the management of those risks that could impact directly.

Part V also considers the importance of emerging risks. Much has been written about emerging risks and the wide range of relevant issues, including climate change, sovereign debt, national security and changing demographics. Emerging risks may be considered in three categories:

1 New risks that have emerged in the external environment, but are associated with the existing strategy of the organization.
2 Existing risks that were already known to the organization but have developed, changed or been triggered.
3 Risks that were not previously faced by the organization because they are linked to new strategy, tactics, operations or compliance requirements.

Although it is possible to separate emerging risks into different categories, there is a common factor. Generally speaking, risks are considered to be emerging risks because the organization does not have sufficient information on the potential impact or anticipated consequences. The governance of emerging risks is, therefore, primarily concerned with the management of the uncertainty associated with not having sufficient information. Governance of emerging risks requires the organization to establish a clear understanding of the rewards associated with the risky activities and decide whether the reward is sufficient.

Scope of risk governance

The scope of risk governance can be demonstrated by use of the risk management bow-tie. This simple diagram, shown in Figure PV, extracts information from the risk management cube shown in Figure I in the Introduction. It incorporates the key messages relevant to effective risk governance.

The risk governance bow-tie illustrates that development of appropriate risk governance activities needs to consider the potential impact of risk events on the finances, infrastructure, reputation and marketplace of the organization. Risk governance activities should also ensure that the organization successfully achieves board oversight of the management of the anticipated consequences of these events for strategy, tactics, operations and compliance.

FIGURE PV Risk governance bow-tie

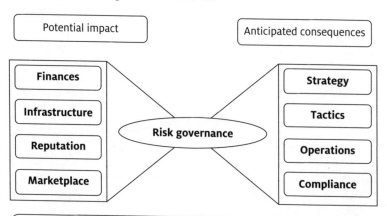

Key messages for Part V

Part V is concerned with risk governance of the organization and includes consideration of the expectations of the wide range of stakeholders. Another important consideration when designing and implementing risk governance arrangements is how the organization will react to emerging risks. These risks may be internal or external to the organization, but the common factor is that insufficient information will be available about the risks. The risk governance arrangements within an organization need to take account of its wide range of stakeholders and their often contradictory expectations, which will give rise to a number of different risk assurance requirements; and organizations should have dynamic procedures in place to be able to respond appropriately to changing or emerging risks; these procedures will need to pay due regard to the rewards that are being sought.

CHAPTER SEVENTEEN

RELEVANCE OF RISK GOVERNANCE

Purpose of corporate governance

Corporate governance is usually defined as the system by which organizations are directed and controlled. In a practical sense, corporate governance involves the two components of governance *of* the board and governance *by* the board. Governance of the board is concerned with issues such as board membership, accountability and remuneration. Governance by the board is concerned with a wide range of activities within the organization.

In terms of risk management activities in an organization, the more important consideration is governance by the board of risk management. The board is responsible for the strategy, tactics, operations and compliance of the organization and has a substantial duty to oversee risk and risk management. The scope of corporate governance in relation to risk will depend on whether the organization undertakes risk activities for passive or proactive reasons. In short, the governance responsibilities should be aligned with the risk agenda for the organization.

Importance of risk governance

Appropriate risk governance is important to all organizations. Below is a brief edited extract from the report and accounts of the Driver and Vehicle Licensing Agency (DVLA), which is part of the Department of Transport in the UK:

The system of internal control is designed to manage risk to a reasonable level rather than to eliminate all risk of failure to achieve policies, aims and objectives. It can, therefore, only provide reasonable and not absolute assurance of effectiveness. The system of internal control is based on a continuing process designed to identify and prioritize the risks to the achievement of policies, aims and objectives and to manage them efficiently, effectively and economically.

We do not try to eliminate all error and fraud with certainty as this would not be a cost-effective or even possible objective. The balance achieved is kept under regular review as circumstances change and new issues arise. The board provides guidance and leadership to managers on how to respond to risks they have identified by owning and managing key risks as well as issuing a risk appetite profile to guide others. The risk appetite is set by the board according to the five categories of risk:

- *Reputation: Cautious (preference for safe options that offer a low degree of residual risk and may offer limited reward).*
- *Operations: Open (willing to consider all potential delivery options and choose one most likely to result in success).*
- *Change programmes: Open.*
- *Finance and value for money: Cautious.*
- *Legal and regulatory: Minimal (choose safe option with low degree of inherent risk).*

All organizations have a wide range of stakeholders with different and often conflicting interests. The management of conflicting interests and the extent to which the expectations of one set of stakeholders are favoured over those of another, represent one of the critical aspects of corporate governance. Although all stakeholders should be treated equitably, the organization will need to decide how to resolve conflicting stakeholder expectations. (The importance of stakeholder expectations is discussed in detail in Chapter 20.)

If a proactive approach is taken to risk management, the corporate governance arrangements should reflect this approach. When an organization takes a proactive approach, there may be investment decisions specifically designed to reduce the level of risk and/or the anticipated consequences should risk events occur. For example, some organizations take the approach that capital expenditure applications should indicate the impact of the investment on the risk profile of the organization. The board will need to be satisfied that the investment will improve the effectiveness and efficiency of activities and processes in the organization.

Corporate governance concerns should extend beyond consideration of investment decisions to the evaluation of business opportunities. In particular, the corporate governance structure should consider the potential for missed opportunities. In relation to risk management, the issue of concern is whether the risk to reward balance is correct. Organizations should invest in projects and tactics that reduce risk and/or improve efficiency; they should also invest in projects and tactics that seize opportunities.

Whether the investment is to improve efficiency or seize opportunities, it needs to be subject to appropriate governance procedures. This is true in all types and sizes of organizations. For many small organizations, governance procedures will be undertaken by banks or other financiers that have received a request to lend money to the organization. The financier will wish to protect its loan or investment and ensure it is not facing an inappropriate credit risk by making an investment in an enterprise that will fail.

Scope of corporate governance activities

The checklist for risk governance is included at the end of this part of the book (see pp 218–219). It provides an indication of the scope of corporate governance activities that are appropriate in all types of organizations. Figure 17.1 provides a simple overview of risk governance components and how it should be aligned with the risk agenda for

FIGURE 17.1 Scope of risk governance

Risk agenda • identify the passive and proactive risk management drivers for the organization • design the features of the risk management initiative for the organization	**Risk assessment** • analyse potential impact to finances, infrastructure, reputation and marketplace • evaluate anticipated consequences for strategy, tactics, operations and compliance

Risk governance
- implement suitable arrangements to provide risk assurance to key stakeholders
- establish robust procedures for the governance of existing and emerging risks

Risk communication • establish the risk architecture, strategy and protocols for the organization • produce a dynamic risk register that describes critical controls and further actions	**Risk response** • implement controls that are preventive, corrective, directive and/or detective • evaluate resilience and devise disaster recovery and business continuity plans

the organization. The figure illustrates that risk governance is required in respect of the risk agenda, risk assessment, risk response and risk communications.

Although risk governance is only a component of the overall governance arrangements, the scope of the risk governance activities should be consistent with the generally accepted principles of corporate governance. The accepted principles of corporate governance include the following:

- promote transparent and efficient markets, be consistent with legal requirements and articulate division of responsibilities;
- protect and facilitate the exercise of the rights of shareholders and ensure equitable treatment of all shareholders;
- recognize the rights of stakeholders and encourage active cooperation in creating wealth, jobs and sustainability;
- ensure timely and accurate disclosure of all material matters, including financial situation, performance, ownership and governance;
- ensure guidance of the company, effective monitoring of management and accountability of the board to the company and shareholders.

To fulfil corporate governance requirements, the board of the organization needs to pay due regard to risk and risk management. The principles listed above should guide corporate governance activities and pay particular attention to the role of risk management. In fulfilling governance responsibilities, the board should pay regard to the relevant risk management aspects of each of these components, as follows:

- *strategy*, by ensuring that the organization has the resources to deliver the desired strategy and has evaluated the risks it is willing to take to achieve the strategy that has been selected;
- *tactics*, by ensuring that the organization has the resources to invest in the tactics that have been selected to deliver the desired strategy and that the risks involved are proportionate to the reward anticipated;
- *operations*, by ensuring that appropriate resources by way of people, premises, processes and products are available to ensure resilience of the organization and these can be ethically and sustainably resourced;
- *compliance*, by ensuring that due regard has been paid to meeting statutory and contractual obligations and plans are in place to meet minimum legal requirements in respect of all aspects of the organization and its activities.

Risk and the three lines of defence

When designing the risk governance structure as part of the risk architecture, the organization may decide on a structure based on the three lines of defence model. This model describes the following allocation of responsibilities:

1 management (and especially top management) has primary responsibility for the management of risk;
2 specialist risk management functions can assist management develop the approach to fulfilling their responsibilities; and
3 the internal audit function checks that the risk management process and framework are effective and efficient.

Management may be divided into the three layers of top management (directors), middle management (managers) and staff or employees. Specialist risk management functions may operate at corporate or group level to develop, implement, monitor and improve the risk management framework. Risk management functions also include specialist experts, such as health and safety and business continuity. These specialist functions fulfil the same role as the group risk management function, but in the more specific area of risk.

Internal audit is primarily concerned with risk assurance, and this will be the concern of the non-executive audit committee in a large organization. Given that internal audit is validating the controls and procedures in place to manage risk, it may be inappropriate for internal auditors to also fulfil an executive function, such as assisting management with the identification, design and implementation of those risk control measures. The three lines of defence model applied within a financial institution is described in the following box.

Three lines of defence

Most financial institutions adopt the three lines of defence approach to operational risk. Operational risk is defined by Basel II as the risk of loss resulting from inadequate or failed internal processes, people and systems, or external events. This encompasses the effectiveness of risk management techniques and controls to minimize these losses.

A typical governance model that deploys three lines of defence will be structured as follows:

1 The first line of defence is the management of the organization and is responsible for the identification and management of operational risks within their respective areas, in line with established policy standards.

2 The second line of defence is the dedicated central operational risk team who are responsible for the provision of a consistent operational risk framework and policy across the group in line with best practice and regulatory expectations, and operate alongside other areas including compliance monitoring, legal and regulatory advice and financial crime management.

3 Internal audit acts as the third line of defence and has independent oversight of the appropriateness and effectiveness of the operational risk framework.

With respect to the role of a senior risk management specialist within the organization, there is no single established reporting position in the structure of an organization for the risk manager. At present, risk managers may report to human resources, the finance director or the company secretary. Sometimes, the risk manager reports to the corporate treasurer and, occasionally, directly to the chief executive officer (CEO). In some cases, the specialist risk management resource may be outsourced. Very simply, the risk manager should be placed in the organization in the best position to be able to deliver the risk agenda.

Although the three lines of defence model may seem excessive for many small organizations, the logic of this approach is compelling. All organizations will have in-house management with responsibility for risk management. Sometimes, smaller organizations realize that they require additional and/or specialist risk management expertise. Often, this will be in relation to health and safety, cyber or other particular risk areas. This outsourced expertise will be the second line of defence, even though it is not employed directly by the organization.

Small organizations will generally not have an in-house internal audit department, nor feel the need to outsource that function to another organization. Nevertheless, the evaluation of internal controls will take place. For a small organization, financial accounts will need to be produced to the satisfaction of the finance professional undertaking the work and/or the financier supporting the business. Although this input is limited to financial controls, it does, nevertheless, operate as a third line of defence.

Therefore, the three lines of defence model will exist in almost all organizations, even if it is not formally described or even recognized. In small organizations, the lines of defence will only be constructed to the extent that is necessary. However, for large complex organizations, is it is possible that the three lines of defence model will be even further developed. Many large organizations will have the second line of defence in-house by way of a risk management department and/or specialist risk management functions such as health and safety, security, fraud/money laundering and business continuity.

The third line of defence may also be an in-house internal audit department or an outsourced audit function. Depending on the size, nature and complexity of an organization, there may be other parties involved in the management of risk. A fourth line of defence may exist by way of external auditors and it is possible that regulators will form a fifth line of defence, in certain types of organizations. Therefore, even in small organizations governance structures will often be more sophisticated than appears to be the case.

Governance and risk management

Corporate governance covers a very wide range of topics and risk management is an integral part of the successful corporate governance of every organization. Most countries impose governance requirements on organizations. These requirements are particularly strong for companies quoted on stock exchanges, organizations that are registered charities, and government departments, agencies and authorities. The purpose of corporate governance is to facilitate accountability and responsibility for efficient and effective performance and ethical behaviour. It should protect executives and employees in undertaking the work they are required to do. Finally, it should ensure stakeholder confidence in the ability of the organization to identify and achieve the outcomes that stakeholders expect.

There are two main approaches to the enforcement of corporate governance standards. Some countries treat corporate governance requirements as 'comply or explain'; in other words, the organization should comply with the principles established by the regulator or explain that they have introduced equivalent or better alternative arrangements. Other countries have a more prescriptive approach that requires full compliance with the established rules. When establishing the risk governance structure for the organization, the board should be aware of stakeholder and regulatory requirements. If the organization operates in a highly regulated environment, it will either be required to adhere to governance principles (comply or explain) or achieve compliance with specific rules. The risk governance structure that the organization puts in place needs to pay due regard to the applicable regulatory framework(s).

The example in the box below considers ethical trading issues at a retail store. This is an example of risk governance input into decisions concerning strategic, tactical, operational and compliance issues. By paying full regard to risk management and corporate governance issues, the retail store will be able to resource merchandise in an ethical and sustainable manner.

Ethical trading at a retail store

When a large retailer decides that it wants all goods for sale to customers to be ethically sourced, it needs to look at the controls that can be placed on suppliers to ensure that it only obtains merchandise from ethically sound sources. The retailer could require the supplier to produce a routine corporate social responsibility report as part of the contract terms and conditions. This report will include the following information:

- details of the policy that the supplier has on ethical behaviour of producers;
- confirmation of the contractual terms and conditions of production;
- statement that producers do not sub-contract work, unless authorized;
- details of staff training, accident/absence rates and pay/conditions;
- results of audits/physical inspection of producer premises.

The retailer can then advertise to customers that all goods are ethically sourced. This will gain good publicity and promote the retailer as having high corporate social responsibility awareness and standards.

Corporate social responsibility is an important aspect of corporate governance in general and risk governance in particular. Positive reporting on corporate social responsibility issues can be a significant benefit for an organization. This will be especially true when it operates in an area where the public is suspicious. The public may not be sympathetic towards a number of organizations because of general perception of the business sector and/or the organization itself.

The importance of corporate social responsibility, ethical trading and sustainability within the supply chain has increased considerably in recent times. Allegations of unethical trading relating to the sourcing of products produced in socially unacceptable working conditions are significant reputational risks. Also, the quality of products and failure to provide value for money can result in damage to reputation and may be associated with unethical trading. As part of the risk governance structure, an organization should make arrangements for governance of the supply chain to ensure that the significant risks have been identified and appropriately managed.

CHAPTER EIGHTEEN

PROVIDING RISK ASSURANCE

Purpose of risk assurance

If risk management activities are undertaken for passive reasons, risk assurance is the primary motivation for doing so. The audit committee will seek assurance that all of the significant risks are being adequately managed and that all of the critical controls are effective and have been efficiently implemented. Even when risk management is undertaken for proactive reasons, risk assurance remains an important component of the overall risk management process.

For organizations that take a passive approach to risk management, the ability to provide risk assurance to the relevant stakeholders will be sufficient. However, for organizations that take a more proactive approach, risk assurance will also be required in relation to the investments being undertaken to improve the efficiency and effectiveness of strategy, tactics, operations and compliance. The required assurance will relate to management of risks within the proposed improvements, as well as an evaluation of the risk to reward return.

The purpose of risk assurance is to provide an objective evaluation of risk management within the organization to the satisfaction of relevant stakeholders. For a small organization, many of the parties requiring risk assurance will be external. In particular, financiers and sponsors will need to be reassured that they are not running an undue credit risk, that the organization will be successful and they will obtain a return on their investment.

Obtaining risk assurance is an important part of the corporate governance arrangements for all organizations, as well as being of benefit to the strategic, project, operational and compliance processes, activities and decisions. The benefits of adequate risk assurance are as follows:

- builds confidence with stakeholders in general and sponsors and financiers in particular;
- helps the organization prevent financial and infrastructure disruption and/or other surprises;
- provides the culture around a framework for enhanced risk awareness and more secure delegation of authority; and
- reduces the chances of damage to reputation and enables the organization to demonstrate good practice to regulators.

Many organizations devise a specific risk assurance strategy that is related to their overall risk management priorities. The risk assurance strategy will be designed to ensure that all parts of the organization assess their risks and maintain appropriate risk registers that are used, as necessary, to drive and monitor risk improvements. The risk assurance strategy is therefore aimed at confirming that the component parts of the organization are correctly implementing the risk management policy. If the risk management policy establishes risk limits, the risk assurance activities will describe how compliance with those limits is confirmed in practice. A typical description of the risk assurance framework for a healthcare trust would be as set out in the following box.

Risk assurance processes

The trust keeps a record of all significant risks, encompassing the 'top down' strategic view of the main risks that threaten the trust and the 'bottom up' operational view of the main risks that threaten the achievement of objectives. The framework is divided into specific areas, aligned to objectives:

- service quality risks, reviewed by the service improvement committee;
- financial risks, reviewed by the audit committee;
- corporate and reputational risks, reviewed by the governance executive;
- clinical risks, reviewed by the clinical risk committee;
- non-clinical risks, reviewed by risk management committee.

The risk architecture shows the flow of information and feedback between the key risk management committees. For each risk there is a full description, the controls in place to minimize the impact or likelihood of the risk and any actions planned to further reduce or eliminate it. The identification of sources of assurance is becoming an increasingly significant aspect of risk management and details include how assurance can be gained that the risk is adequately controlled.

Sources of risk assurance

A wide range of stakeholders in an organization will seek assurance regarding the risk management activities within that organization. Perhaps the most common form of risk assurance is when the board or audit committee of a large company seek assurance from the individual business units that risk and risk management have received appropriate attention. The range of sources of assurance available in these circumstances includes:

- audit reports produced by internal audit and external auditors on a range of issues including risk assessment, implementation, compliance and training;
- business unit reports on such issues as self-assessment reports, response to audit reports and recommendations and reports on incidents that have occurred;
- business performance of the unit on risk-related issues, significant weaknesses in control measures and details of any material losses;
- business unit documentation, such as the risk management policy, risk committee minutes, health and safety policy, disaster recovery and business continuity plans.

Additionally, the board and audit committee will seek external sources of assurance. For example, if the organization faces risks associated with foreign exchange rates, interest rates and/or credit risks, it will identify appropriate leading indicators. If foreign exchange rates or interest rates are stable, the organization will treat this information as a source of assurance regarding future success and profitability. The use of external leading indicators is considered further in the box below.

Examples of risk indicators

The final means of challenging the assurances provided is that the organization has to track external indicators. For example, a large retailer will need to gain an accurate view of the health of the economy in the countries in which it operates. Therefore, such a company will monitor national performance indicators that give a guide to the changing nature of the risks it faces and how these could impact future business success. Such a large retailer may monitor the following:

- unemployment rates;
- inflation rates;
- interest rates;
- house price movements;
- gross domestic product.

The organization may decide that the reports from internal audit and the quality of reports from departments will be the basis of risk assurance. The company can also introduce a self-assessment process that requires the business unit, location or department to provide assurance that significant risks have been identified and are adequately controlled. Areas of weakness identified in the self-assessment returns will be reported to the executive committee and remedial action will be required.

Depending on the risk priorities of the organization, the board or audit committee may require annual reports on certain risks. For example, because of the importance of health and safety at work, boards usually receive annual reports on safety performance. Likewise, the audit committee will wish to receive an annual report on the incidents of fraud that have been detected within the organization. This will be especially true of organizations that handle large amounts of cash such as shops, casinos, cafes and bars.

Risks that are concerned with uncertainty and, in particular, the successful completion of projects, are often the subject of a review by the board or audit committee. Within large organizations, it is typical to have a post-implementation review of a project. For example, if the board of a retail company has authorized the opening of a new store, the audit committee will require a review of the completion of the project. This post-implementation review will evaluate whether the project was delivered on time, within budget and to specification. The review is also likely to report on the first 12 months trading of the new store.

Nature of risk assurance reports

The nature of risk assurance reports will depend on the risk agenda for the organization and the particular group of stakeholders that is requiring assurance. For organizations that are undertaking risk management activities for passive or assurance reasons, the risk assurance report would be a fairly simple document that provides a snapshot of the status of risk and risk management within the organization. Such a report may also be sufficient for some external stakeholders.

However, unless the reason for producing the risk assurance report has been clearly established, there is a danger that too much information will be included. If the approach of the audit committee is to look for assurance that all significant risks have been identified and appropriate controls are in place, a simple report will suffice. If the organization is seeking to produce a risk governance report that is designed to provide assurance and is not intended to report on improvements in risk exposure, it may be sufficient to provide a report with the following sections:

- risk management framework and overall approach to risk;
- narrative description of the current status of the significant risks;
- analysis of these risks in terms of probability, impact and mitigating actions;
- anticipated consequences for strategy, tactics, operations and compliance;
- changes to the risk profile since the previous risk governance report.

This simple risk governance report will be sufficient and may be prepared by the executive committee, evaluated by the audit committee and finally presented to the board. However, this approach is only likely to be sufficient if the organization is taking a passive or assurance approach to risk management. This may be perfectly satisfactory in a small organization where the executive committee is already familiar with the risks and the level of control. The passive approach will mean that the organization is not seeking to improve risk management performance so much as to confirm that risks and risk management receive appropriate attention.

When an organization takes a more proactive approach to risk management, a more comprehensive risk report will be appropriate. The complexity of this report will depend on how well aligned and embedded risk management activities are. If risk information is provided as part of the mainstream of management information, a separate risk management report becomes unnecessary. Development from the simple risk assurance report to a position where risk management is fully integrated within main management information streams may take some time to achieve. In these circumstances, key risk indicators may become indistinguishable from the key performance indicators that are used by the organization to measure and improve overall success.

Challenging assurances offered

It is not sufficient for the board or audit committee to simply accept the risk assurances that are provided by business units. It will be particularly important to challenge the assurances when they are given as a self-assessment report. The audit committee will be able to evaluate the quality of reports and decide whether they provide sufficient assurance on the status of risk management within that business unit. By asking questions of the business unit, location or department, as well as challenging internal audit reports, the audit committee will be able to gain an objective view of how seriously the business unit takes risk management.

Importance of challenging assurances

Many organizations recognize the need to challenge the assurances that are provided at the audit committee. There is also a need to challenge the objectives that are often used as the means of identifying risks in the first place. Here is an edited extract from the Cambridgeshire Police Authority Risk management strategy:

Our working definition of a risk is an uncertainty or the chance of something happening – an event, a change in circumstances or a consequence – which can have an impact on objectives and priorities. These may be negative or a deviation from the expected. This definition links risks to objectives, so this definition can most readily be applied when the objectives of the organization are comprehensive and fully stated. Even then the objectives need to be challenged and the underlying assumptions tested as part of the risk management process.

Part of the ability to challenge risk assurances will be based on the performance of the business unit. In relation to assurances given to financiers, the actual performance of the organization is likely to be the main criterion on which risk performance is measured. However, there is a danger that good performance by a business unit may be a direct result of taking too much risk and/or having insufficient controls in place. If the performance of the business unit is used to provide risk assurance, the board or audit committee will need to challenge the accuracy of the performance that is reported.

When seeking assurance, the board or audit committee will require confirmation that the business unit is paying due regard to risk management responsibilities. Internal auditors will form an opinion on this and will be able to provide an informal report to the board or audit committee. However, a more formal and objective approach is sometimes required and this can be obtained by seeking to measure the risk culture of the business unit. The purpose of doing so within a business unit is to enable the audit committee to evaluate the extent to which the risk agenda for the organization is likely to be implemented within that unit.

Another means for the audit committee to challenge the assurances given is to evaluate the information provided against targets that have been set. If the organization has introduced measurable loss control or other risk management programmes, these will include key performance indicators, sometimes referred to as 'risk indicators'. By introducing direct risk measures, the level of assurance provided can be directly related to the level of risk exposure and/or loss experience and the targets that have been set.

If this approach is taken, the organization should check that the performance indicators are relevant to the success of the business, rather than a measure of reducing the potential impact of risks to finances, infrastructure, reputation and marketplace. To be fully relevant, risk performance indicators should be a measure of business success and included in the same management information stream as other business performance indicators.

Using such indicators may be disproportionate for many smaller organizations. In that case, these organizations will monitor the performance indicators that are relevant to their own particular activities. For example, a supplier of steelwork to the construction industry will want to monitor the price of steel and the economic activity within the construction sector. In this example, the price of steel is an external leading indicator that gives early warning of a change in the level of risk, whereas the level of economic activity in the sector is a lagging indicator, giving information on past performance.

Identifying and monitoring suitable leading and lagging indicators will help challenge assurances that are given on risk performance. If the unit supplies steelwork to the construction industry, the audit committee will be in a better position to challenge any assurance about the future performance of the business unit if movements in the price of steel and the rate of economic activity in the construction sector have been separately investigated by the audit committee.

An important part of challenging risk assurances is to identify the assumptions that underpin the success of the business unit, location or department. For example, a mortgage company may have a business model that depends on the availability of funds on the wholesale money markets, rather than depending on money being deposited by individual savers. In these circumstances, if the wholesale money markets are unable to provide funds, the business model will fail. Therefore, to accept the assurances provided by the business unit, the board or audit committee will need to understand the business model and challenge the assumption that the wholesale money markets will always function as anticipated.

CHAPTER NINETEEN

GOVERNANCE OF EMERGING RISKS

Nature of emerging risks

Several recent corporate failures have been blamed on emerging risks. These are often described as the high impact low likelihood risks that are sometimes seen as being impossible to predict. The analysis is that the risks were so unlikely that they could not be foreseen and, therefore, management could not be held responsible for the consequences. The ITV case study included at the end of Part I indicates that the company has analysed the high impact, low likelihood risks and has taken steps to plan the reaction if the risks were to occur (see pp 50–51).

All organizations are concerned about changes in the external and internal context that give rise to new challenges, uncertainties and, perhaps, opportunities. These changes can be considered to be the emerging risks they face, and organizations need to clearly understand their nature. Emerging risks can be divided into three categories:

1 new risks in the external environment that are associated with the existing strategy of the organization – new risks in known context;
2 existing risks already known to the organization but that have significantly increased or been triggered – known risks in new context;
3 risks not previously faced by the organization because they are associated with new strategy, tactics, operations or compliance – new risks in new context.

Although this analysis is correct, it may be better to focus on emerging risks as those risks where insufficient information is available. For many organizations, emerging risks will relate to cyber risks, supply chain risks and/or project risks. Project risks can be thought of as: 1) risks associated with the selection of an inappropriate project, and 2) risks associated with the delivery of the project.

Several business developments have increased the level of risk faced by organizations in recent times, including moving into new markets, embracing new technologies and developing increasingly complex supply chains. Generally, these increasing risks will be under the control of the organization itself. Additionally, there are many sovereign and/or global emerging or developing risks that are not within the control of an individual organization, including climate change, sovereign debt, national security and changing demographics.

A good example of emerging risk is nanotechnology. Nanotechnology is used extensively in the medical and, to some extent, cosmetics industry to improve the effectiveness of cosmetic treatment of skin conditions. Whether any long-term risks will emerge from the use of nanotechnology has not yet been fully established. This example reinforces the view that emerging risks are simply those risks where insufficient information is available to the organization.

If a chain of retail shops opens a new store in a location where it has not previously traded, it may not have all the necessary information on spending patterns in the area. However, other retailers in that location will be aware of those spending patterns and will have sufficient information to be able to stock appropriate products. The organization opening the new store may believe that expanding into a new location is an emerging risk. It is more helpful to think of the risks as arising from insufficient information: when the risk is identified this way, the organization can undertake due diligence to discover the required information.

Responding to emerging risks

Management and the board of an organization are responsible for the strategy, tactics, operations and compliance of that organization. The explanation to stakeholders that something unexpected happened and management cannot be held responsible for the consequences of these emerging risks is not sufficient. Organizations that take a proactive approach to risk management will constantly be aware of their changing risk profile and looking to devise appropriate responses, and/or obtain further information, on a continuous basis.

Proactive management of the risks facing an organization involves trying to predict emerging risks and taking actions to limit the anticipated consequences. Also, this proactive approach to risk and risk management should put the organization in a position of being able to not only respond to emerging risks, but also to gain benefit from viewing these emerging risks as opportunities to develop the business, thus gaining a competitive advantage and/or being able to deliver products and services in a more efficient and effective manner.

Responding to emerging risks

Many organizations are concerned about the emergence of what appear to be new risks within the local and/or global business environment. These emerging risks include terrorism, global disease, extreme weather events, cyber risk and the increasing complexity of the supply chain.

Some risks emerge rapidly with devastating effects. These include earthquakes, tsunamis and extreme weather events. Other risks are associated with threats that may not materialize for a particular organization, such as terrorism, global disease and cyber risk. Perhaps these emerging risks are more accurately considered to be uncertainties and/or risks for which inadequate information is available.

However these risks are defined, it appears that the most effective responses are based on scenario planning and ensuring that crisis plans are in place. Crisis plans included disaster recovery and business continuity plans.

To be in a better position to predict the potential impact of emerging risks, an organization needs to identify leading indicators that will help determine both the potential impact and anticipated consequences. The difficulty for many organizations is that there may be inadequate knowledge about an emerging risk. Without this, it is not possible to undertake an accurate risk assessment. If critical knowledge is missing or unavailable, the risk may be ignored or overlooked and the potential impact can become greater and/or more likely.

An important consideration when thinking about emerging risks is the speed at which they can become significant. This is sometimes referred to as 'risk speed' or 'risk velocity'. Responding to changing circumstances is a key responsibility of top management of the organization and regular risk assessment of strategy, tactics, operations and compliance should identify gradual changes. However, if the emerging risk develops rapidly, more urgent plans are required. In some circumstances, the organization will need to develop disaster recovery and business continuity plans to respond to rapidly emerging risks, as described in Chapter 11.

Examples of emerging risks

Examples of emerging risks have been mentioned earlier in this chapter. Two of the most rapidly developing risks for organizations are related to cyber risk exposures and supply chain and/or outsourcing risks. Cyber risk exposures can arise from failure to fulfil obligations to third parties and because of failure of computers, communications or other electronic equipment. The box below provides an example of changing cyber risk exposures for a typical organization.

Changing cyber risk exposures

Many organizations are willing to transfer their data storage arrangements to a third party that provides the storage facilities 'in the cloud' – an example of outsourcing of a vitally important component of the organization. Using a cloud service provider is also an example of setting up a supply chain and adding complexity to the infrastructure of the organization. By outsourcing the storage of data to a third party the organization will be seeking advantages, including:

- reduction in investment in IT hardware and increased flexibility and increased investment available for the core business;
- access to global networks and superior technology, with improved service and wider range of services available;

- increased reliability of the service and reduced need to design and implement IT disaster recovery planning; and
- reduction in number of direct employees and increased certainty in the cost of operating IT systems.

Transferring responsibility for the management of computer data to a third party changes the nature of the cyber risk exposures faced by the organization. These may be seen as emerging risks, but this example simply demonstrates the benefits of considering emerging risks as those risks where insufficient information is available. Also, the example of outsourcing data storage demonstrates that risks cannot be fully transferred to a third party. If the outsourced service provider fails in its responsibilities to protect third-party data or fails to provide a sufficiently continuous service, the organization will still suffer.

Outsourcing of the various components of the infrastructure of an organization is a part of supply chain management, successful management of which will rely on strategic partnerships and may also extend to joint-venture arrangements. Supply chain issues also include simple outsourcing decisions, such as the appointment of external cleaners and caterers.

The scope of the supply chain can be very extensive and includes strategic partnerships, joint ventures, support services and outsourcing of facilities management activities. Many organizations also choose to outsource the transport component of their business. It is not unusual for chains of retail stores to outsource warehousing arrangements and the delivery of goods to their individual shops. However, a careful evaluation of the balance between risk and reward should be undertaken before any supply chain outsourcing decisions are taken.

Supply chain considerations become even more important when production activities are involved. When a chain store sets up an arrangement for the supply of manufactured goods, the ability of the supply chain partner to deliver the required goods on time, within the agreed cost and on a sustainable and ethical basis will be key considerations.

When an organization does not have sufficient resources to embrace a new business strategy, or it does not find the level of risk involved in that new strategy tolerable, it may consider setting up a joint venture with the existing supplier. Setting up joint ventures also allows the organization to have some management control over the operation of that supplier and eliminate the possibility that the supplier will deliver goods to a competitor in difficult market conditions. Setting up a new joint venture to take advantage of a developing opportunity could be evaluated as an emerging risk of the organization.

Joint-venture arrangements may also be an appropriate way of responding to competitor activities by denying the competitor access to the products from the supplier that is now a joint-venture partner. Joint ventures may also be a successful way of responding to technology changes in the marketplace, because the organization will not need to find all of the funding required to respond. The advantage of joint ventures is that the risks are shared and, accordingly, the benefits and rewards will be shared. These are usually shared by contractual agreements or by setting up a separate company with an agreed allocation of capital to fund that company.

Challenges of emerging risks

The ability to manage emerging risks will improve as more information about the risks becomes available. Therefore, the key to managing emerging risks is obtaining the required information and, consequently, good communication is essential. As the scope of the emerging risk becomes clear, the best way of responding also becomes more obvious. However, organizations do not always have the time or resources to obtain all of the information they would like to have before making important strategic decisions.

The skill required of management when dealing with emerging risks is to make correct decisions based on incomplete, or sometimes inaccurate, information. Sometimes relevant data can be obtained by identifying appropriate leading risk indicators and monitoring their performance. In most cases, the leading risk indicator will provide information on the potential impact of the emerging risk. The challenge for management is to use this information to correctly evaluate the anticipated consequences for the organization.

Many tactics are available to manage emerging risks. The options of outsourcing, strategic partnerships and joint ventures have been considered earlier in this chapter. The important consideration is that implementing tactics will require the organization to undertake a project and/or a programme of work. The tactics selected will be designed to ensure that the organization develops and maintains effective and efficient operations. Tactics may need to be developed in the absence of adequate risk information and the judgement of top management will be required when deciding how to respond to an emerging risk. It is also clear that this same level of judgement is required of top management when they are deciding what tactics to adopt to correctly respond to an emerging opportunity.

A further example of an emerging risk that many organizations have been facing is the financial implications of increased life expectancy for the pension fund, as described in the box below. This is often referred to as 'longevity risk' and it is the risk that individuals live longer than anticipated, with consequent increased demands on pension funds. The uncertainty about future life expectancy poses a serious financial threat to individuals, employers that sponsor pension funds and governments. The longevity risk can result in pensioner poverty and calls on governments to meet shortfalls.

Longevity risk and pension funds

Global longevity risk exposure is very substantial. As life expectancy increases and awareness of the financial risk increases, there will be a growing demand for longevity risk mitigation solutions. Life insurers have an important role to play in providing indemnity for longevity risk. However, their current capacity to take longevity risk onto the balance sheet may be inadequate. Developing solutions to transfer longevity risk to the capital markets can help.

All stakeholders in longevity risk will benefit from investor and population awareness of the risk, access to reliable population data to help model and quantify the risk and regulation that promotes a rigorous risk-based capital framework for both insurers and pension funds.

Any solutions to the longevity risk are likely to be financially sophisticated and will require some financial commitment from the organization. The design and implementation of a suitable solution to the longevity risk will require careful project planning that incorporates detailed risk assessment. The risk assessment will require financial modelling that may often be based on inadequate data to allow an accurate calculation of the financial implications for the organization.

CHAPTER TWENTY

RISK AND STAKEHOLDER EXPECTATIONS

Identifying the range of stakeholders

There is a growing recognition that analysis of stakeholder expectations provides a very useful basis for planning risk management activities. Some stakeholders will simply require information about the organization and others will require assurance regarding risk management activities. Also, some stakeholders may place mandatory requirements on an organization in respect of its risk management activities. All of these stakeholder expectations are aligned with the passive approach to risk management undertaken in many organizations. These are likely to be the stakeholders in the finances, infrastructure, reputation and marketplace of the organization.

Other stakeholders will require a more proactive approach and these are likely to be the stakeholders in the strategy, tactics, operations and compliance of the organization. These stakeholders are likely to (additionally) require continuous improvement in performance from the organization; this is aligned with the effectiveness and efficiency of processes within the organization.

Different stakeholders will have different expectations of the organization. There will be a wide range of different groups of stakeholders and these can be summarized as follows, together with an indication of why the organization should be interested in the expectations of those stakeholders:

- Customers are the ultimate consumers of the products and/or services and provide funding for established commercial organizations.
- Staff provide the human resources without which the organization would not be able to produce products or deliver services.
- Financiers provide the capital, especially during the start-up phase and their importance is focused on the funding of tactics.
- Suppliers provide the products and services that the organization depends on to produce its own outputs.
- Regulators control the organization and may be in a position to withdraw a licence that allows the organization to operate.
- Society gains economic benefit from the organization, but will require fair and ethical treatment of all stakeholders.

Different stakeholders will have contradictory expectations of the organization. For example, staff at a sports club will want pay that is as high as possible; this would be in opposition to the requirements of financiers, who want the club to be as profitable as possible. It is an important part of the role of top management to evaluate the conflicting interests of different stakeholders and implement actions that provide the best balance between stakeholder expectations.

For some energy companies, environmental pressure groups are often unwelcome stakeholders. There may be a substantial conflict between a mining company that wants to extract minerals and the local population who do not want heavy industrial activities taking place in the area. (Managing the conflicting expectations of stakeholders is considered in the case study of Organate Foods in Appendix 1.) The importance of communicating with different stakeholder groups, together with the responsibility for ensuring appropriate communications take place, is referred to in the case studies at the end of this part of the book; see pp 220–223.

Identifying stakeholders and their expectations is vitally important. In fact, there is a trend in risk management towards treating stakeholders and their expectations as a starting point for risk assessment. There is no doubt that failure to deliver stakeholder expectations represents a significant risk. By identifying the range of important stakeholders in an organization, it is possible to identify their expectations and manage the events that would undermine the delivery of those expectations.

Responding to stakeholder expectations

By identifying, analysing and evaluating stakeholder expectations, the risk agenda becomes more relevant to the success of the organization. Analysing the potential impact of events on finances, infrastructure, reputation and marketplace provides good understanding of the events that could have a significant impact. The more important question in terms of the success of the organization is the anticipated consequences of those events for strategy, tactics, operations and compliance.

The risk assessment exercise will focus on the analysis of the potential impact to finances, infrastructure, reputation and marketplace. However, it is probably true to say that stakeholder expectations will more easily be identified in relation to strategy, tactics, operations and compliance. Regulators, for example, have a direct link with the level of compliance achieved by the organization. Staff and customers will more easily identify with the operations of the organization and the people, premises, processes and products that are involved in these operations. The ability to more easily attach stakeholder expectations to strategy, tactics, operations and compliance demonstrates the relevance of considering stakeholder expectations when undertaking risk management activities.

Responding to stakeholder expectations

It can be seen that there is a wide range of stakeholders in most organizations. Some of these stakeholders may be unwanted as far as the organization is concerned. The risk governance arrangements of the organization should include details of responsibilities for communicating with stakeholders, including those who might object to the strategy and tactics of the organization, as well as regulators who may be willing to grant licences and authority for the organization to implement the strategy and tactics.

For example, if a distribution company wants to build an extension to its depot, local residents may object to it on the basis of increased noise and traffic problems in the immediate area. The local residents are stakeholders in the operation of the company, even though the owner of the company may not want to acknowledge that fact.

A particular consideration in relation to stakeholder expectations is the management of projects. Generally speaking, the stakeholders in a project will be the organization that commissioned it, the financiers and, ultimately, the end-users. During delivery of the project itself, the key stakeholders are the organization, contractors and financiers. Expectations in relation to timescale, cost and quality can be more readily assigned to the individual stakeholders and plans put in place to deliver those expectations. The relative importance of stakeholders and the desire of the organization to fulfil their expectations will help define the risk management priorities during delivery of the project.

As the project is progressing, the risk events that could occur can be identified and managed in a way that is fully documented and fully embedded within the management of the project. In simple terms, the identification of stakeholder expectations represents a very robust way of identifying the risks associated with the project. Project risks include the risk that it is the wrong project and the risk that the project is not delivered effectively. There will, of course, be different stakeholders and different stakeholder expectations in relation to these two sets of risks.

Stakeholder risk expectations

Consideration needs to be given to the relative importance of stake-holders as part of deciding how to manage their conflicting interests. It may be useful to analyse the list of stakeholders in the organization and review their separate expectations. It is important that organiza-tions retain the support of all stakeholders, if possible, and to do this the organization may need to be proactive in its approach to risk manage-ment and identify the stakeholder expectations in advance. By doing this, it will be possible to manage stakeholder expectations, either by delivering them in full or by providing sufficient information and justi-fication for failing to deliver those expectations to the extent that the particular stakeholder required.

Core processes deliver stakeholder expectations and they are related to the aim, mission and objectives of the organization. (The nature and importance of core processes is discussed in more detail in Chapter 7.) Since core processes deliver stakeholder expectations, a risk can be defined as an event with the potential to impact the delivery of core processes or fulfilment of a stakeholder expectation. This approach has the advantage that both internal and external stakeholders can be identified, together with their short-, medium- and long-term expectations.

An approach based on stakeholder expectations has many advantages. It facilitates a full and thorough validation of the core processes of the organization in relation to the expectations that each stakeholder places on each core process. An important aspect of managing an organization is balancing the various stakeholder expectations. There are dangers inherent in achieving this balance, and a risk identification process is the most robust way of ensuring that risks are identified, analysed and evaluated. The box below illustrates the importance placed by some organizations on the fulfilment of the risk management expectations of stakeholders.

Responding to stakeholder risk expectations

The importance of fulfilling the risk management expectations of stakeholders is fully recognized. Here is an edited extract from the risk management policy statement of Cardiff Council:

Cardiff Council is committed to a proactive approach to risk management which is integrated into the policy framework, planning and budgeting cycles. The council recognizes the value of adopting a risk management culture and will seek to identify, analyse, manage and control the risks it faces. The council is committed to the management of risk in order to:

1 *Ensure that statutory obligations and policy objectives are met.*
2 *Prioritize areas for improvement in service provision and encourage meeting or exceeding customer and stakeholder expectations.*
3 *Safeguard its employees, clients or service users, members, pupils, tenants and all other persons to whom the council has a duty of care.*
4 *Protect its property including buildings, equipment, vehicles, knowledge and all other assets and resources.*
5 *Identify and manage potential liabilities.*
6 *Maintain effective control of public funds and efficient deployment and use of resources.*
7 *Preserve and promote the reputation of the council.*
8 *Support the quality of the environment.*

These aims will be attained by systematically identifying, analysing and evaluating, cost effectively controlling and monitoring risks at strategic, programme, project and operational levels.

Although the analysis of stakeholder expectations can be one of the most robust ways of identifying risks, there are implications in terms of the time and effort required for this approach to be successful. However, the benefits of taking a core processes approach include the ability to identify the core processes that are most vulnerable to risk events. This will enable the identification of stakeholders whose expectations are most likely to be unfulfilled.

If the tactics of an organization involve improvements to products, investment in new production techniques, response to technological changes and/or other developments that require a project, finance is likely to be required. This means that financial bodies are likely to be key stakeholders in projects and similar tactical changes. Other stakeholders in projects may include building contractors and providers of specialist professional support, such as architects.

There may be many stakeholder groups involved in the operational activities of an organization. To use the example of a football club, fans will be major stakeholders in a large number of different aspects of the club's activities. One of the primary concerns of fans will be good results on the pitch. They will also be interested in other operational aspects, including the arrangements for buying tickets, transport and access, as well as the facilities provided within the stadium.

Regulators are the most influential of stakeholders in compliance issues, although banks may also extend influence. Again using the example of a football club, many countries require that sports venues acquire several certificates and licences before they can operate. These may include a licence for the venue, a fire certificate, as well as licences to serve food, alcohol and organize social events.

For all organizations, financiers and sponsors are key stakeholders. They will have expectations of the organization in terms of the return on the money invested. Suppliers will have expectations of fair treatment, including prompt payment of invoices. Although it may be a significant exercise, there is no doubt that a fully comprehensive list of risks will be produced if organizations start their risk identification exercise with an analysis of stakeholder expectations. Figure 7.1 on page 78 offers further consideration.

PART V REVIEW

Checklist

This checklist for risk governance provides a list of four items that should be reviewed to confirm that appropriate risk governance activities have been developed and implemented. The starting point for developing an appropriate approach to risk governance is to complete a riskiness index, described in Chapter 1, and analyse the extent to which risk events could have a potential impact on finances, infrastructure, reputation or marketplace.

The overall objective of risk governance activities is to ensure that the organization has arrangements in place to provide stakeholders with risk assurance. The provision of risk assurance will include confirmation that the organization is undertaking the risk management activities that are mandated by customers and/or regulators. Risk assurance will also ensure that the company is able to confirm that the significant risks to the organization have been identified and managed to the appropriate level.

Risk assurance activities are passive in nature in that they do not seek to improve the risk performance of the organization; an example of the passive approach is the collection of risk information that will be used in decision-making processes. Organizations should also take a proactive approach to risk management to improve the efficiency and effectiveness of strategy, tactics, operations and compliance.

This leads to the second objective of risk governance activities, which is to provide the organization with information on emerging risks. These emerging risks may arise because the business environment has changed and/or the organization is undertaking new activities. The main feature of any emerging risk is that the organization does not have sufficient information about it. Sometimes, decisions have to be taken before all of the information is available. The risk governance structure should ensure that risk decisions are always taken based on the best available information and that they are appropriate given the nature of the reward that is sought.

The checklist below is intended to focus on the priority risk management activities for an organization that is designing and implementing a comprehensive risk management initiative. The checklist sets out the issues relevant to risk governance that need to be clarified by the organization.

1 Describe the arrangements to ensure adequate governance of the significant risks facing the organization, including details of how acceptable levels of risk are determined; who is responsible for implementing those standards; and how achievement of the standards is assured.

2 Describe the mechanisms for achieving assurance regarding the management of the significant risks faced by the organization, including details of how these assurances are obtained, arrangements for challenging these assurances and the risk indicators that are monitored.

3 Evaluate the arrangements in place for the management of emerging risks, including details of the reasons for the lack of information on these risks and the actions that will be taken to obtain the information and/or reduce exposure to the associated uncertainty.

4 Validate the risk management architecture, strategy and protocols in relation to the range of stakeholder expectations in order to ensure that the risk agenda for the organization is appropriate, delivers intended benefits to stakeholders and is not based on any unreliable assumptions.

Case studies

Heriot Watt University: risk management policy

Risk responsibilities

It is essential that all participants in risk management are aware of their roles in the overall process and their own responsibilities.

University Court

The court has responsibility for the total risk exposure of the university by:

- setting the tone and influence of the culture of risk management across the university;
- determining the extent to which the university is 'risk taking' or 'risk averse' and as a whole sets the risk tolerance line for the university;
- approving major decisions affecting the risk profile and/or risk exposure of the university;
- determining what types of risk are acceptable/not acceptable and monitoring significant risks and control improvements to mitigate risks;
- annually reviewing the approach to risk management and approving changes or improvements to key elements of the process and procedures.

To aid this, the court will receive an annual report from internal audit on the effectiveness of the risk management process in the university, making recommendations when necessary.

Planning and management executive

The planning and management executive, advised by the director of finance, is responsible for corporate risks by:

- identifying and evaluating the significant risks faced by the university;
- providing adequate information in a timely manner to the court on the status of risks and controls;

- participating biannually in a risk review and reporting the outcomes to the court;
- implementing policies on risk management and internal control;
- reviewing school, institute, section and project major risks;
- participating in the annual review of effectiveness of the system of internal control and risk management by internal audit.

Schools, institutes and sections

Heads of schools, institutes and sections, supported by their management groups, are responsible for the management and monitoring of risk within their areas of responsibility. School, institute and section risks will be handled in a manner similar to that at university strategy level.

Risk management strategy group

The risk owner has responsibility for monitoring and managing their individual risk. The strategic risk register clearly documents the risk owner along with other relevant information on the risk and therefore each owner is required to be familiar with the risk register. The risk owner is also responsible for the implementation of the measures taken in respect of each risk.

Director of finance

The director of finance and the group risk manager, as the risk process owner, ensures that risk is managed effectively at all levels and that risk registers are reported at an appropriate level.

(Based on information on the Heriot Watt University website 2012.)

Rexham plc: risk remediation

Rexham is committed to protecting the human rights of everyone who works for the company and of all those who have dealings with it. As a responsible company, we support the United Nations universal declaration of human rights that sets 'common standards of achievement for all people and all nations'. We recognize that our responsibility for human rights and labour conditions encompasses:

- Operating sites: in developed countries, performance on most of the issues covered by the human rights and labour conditions policy will be required by law. Therefore, this policy is primarily provided to guide operations in those emerging markets where concerns are regularly expressed about human rights.
- Supply chain: it is our aim that the working conditions throughout our supply chain meet internationally accepted standards of human rights and working conditions.
- Responsibility: we believe that everyone in our organization is responsible for having due regard for human rights. In particular:
  - the board has overall responsibility for ensuring that human rights considerations are integral in the way in which existing operations and new opportunities are developed and managed;
  - managers and supervisors provide visible leadership that promote human rights as an equal priority to other business issues. They also have a responsibility for identifying abuses that occur;
  - all employees are responsible for ensuring that their own actions do not impair the human rights of others. They are also encouraged to bring forward, in confidence, any concerns that they may have about human rights abuses.

We recognize that from time to time we will encounter challenges on human rights that are bigger than Rexham is able to tackle alone. Many human rights abuses are systemic in their host communities. We are therefore committed to working with other organizations that can help us implement the human rights and labour conditions policy effectively over time. Each sector is responsible for ensuring that it has in place the necessary arrangements to monitor and report compliance against the provisions of the policy on an annual basis.

(Edited extract from Rexham plc Global Reporting Initiative (GRI) 2011.)

Interior Services Group: corporate governance

The reporting systems include formal consideration of all significant business risks at monthly board meetings and are subject to continuous review. The monthly management information includes key risk indicators with emphasis on early warning systems. Risk management principles are embedded within all significant projects.

The key risk management activities are described under the following headings:

- Strategic control – the board reviews the strategic plans of the group each year and monitors progress throughout the year. On a regular basis, the significant group risks are updated and appropriate control strategies and accountabilities are agreed.
- Allocation of responsibilities and control environment – the board has set clear terms of reference for each of its committees and the group has an organizational structure with clear reporting lines for financial results, risk exposure and control assessment.
- Quality and integrity of personnel – the group is committed to competence and integrity of management and staff at all levels, through its values statement, comprehensive recruitment, training and appraisal programmes.
- Role of the executive directors – day-to-day management of the activities of the group is delegated by the board to the executive directors. They monitor the effectiveness of the operating units in meeting group objectives and controlling major business risks.
- Risk management reporting and board review – the board has overall responsibility for identifying, evaluating and managing major business risks facing the group.
- Operating unit controls – key controls over major business risks include reviews against performance indicators and exception reporting. Each operating unit is responsible for identifying, evaluating and managing major business risks.
- Financial control – the group has a comprehensive system for reporting financial results to the board. The performance of each business is reviewed monthly by local and group management.
- Internal audit – while there is no dedicated internal audit function, internal audit resources are provided by the central functions and these are considered to be sufficient by the group.

(Edited extract from Interior Services Group Annual Report and Accounts 2011.)

Further reading

BSI (2011) *British Standard BS 31100 (2011): Risk Management. Code of practice and guidance for the implementation of BS ISO 31000*, www.standardsuk.com

COSO (2004) *Enterprise Risk Management – Integrated framework, executive summary*, www.coso.org

Financial Reporting Council (2005) *Internal Control. Revised guidance for directors on the Combined Code*, www.frc.org.uk.

HM Treasury (2004) *Orange Book, Management of risk – principles and concepts*, www.hm-treasury.gov.uk

Hopkin, P (2012) *Fundamentals of Risk Management*, ISBN 978-0-7494-6539-1, Kogan Page: www.koganpage.com

Institute of Chartered Accountants in England and Wales (2002) *Risk Management for SMEs*, www.icaew.com

Institute of Risk Management (2002) *A Risk Management Standard*, www.theirm.org

Institute of Risk Management (2010) *Structured Approach to Enterprise Risk Management and the Requirements of ISO 31000*, www.theirm.org

Risk management and Organate Foods

Introduction to the case study

Organate Foods is a business that grows, imports, sells and delivers organic fruit and vegetables directly to the public in weekly 'veggie boxes'. The business prides itself on sustainable and ethical growing and sourcing of a wide variety of organically grown products from around the world.

The company has been in existence for 30 years and currently has a turnover of £2 million. The board of Organate Foods has the founder as non-executive chairman, together with her son in the role of executive general manager. The two other executive members of the board are the operations manager and the commercial manager. Formal board meetings take place every three months, although there is informal contact between board members on an almost daily basis.

In broad terms, the three executive managers have structured their responsibilities, as follows:

- the general manager is responsible for coordinating the activities of Organate Foods and has specific responsibility for relationships with regulators and financiers;
- the operations manager is responsible for all aspects of crop production and this includes specific responsibility for relationships with staff and neighbours/society;
- the commercial manager is responsible for marketing and sales, as well as all commercial relationships, including suppliers and customers.

Mission of Organate Foods

The company recognizes that the market for organic foods is changing and demand has reduced over the past five years. The very poor weather conditions during the current year resulted in disruption to planting and crop care schedules, as well as poor and/or failed crops and an increase in crop disease. These recent developments have persuaded the board of Organate Foods to review their strategy and tactics for the next five years including paying greater attention to risk management.

The overall mission remains that Organate Foods wishes to deliver a wide range of quality organic fruit and vegetables to domestic customers by way of weekly 'veggie boxes'. The board realizes that the tactics to be employed to deliver this strategy need to be reviewed. In particular, there is a desire to grow a wider range of vegetables on their own land and/or establish a network of local organic growers and suppliers. These tactics require greater diversification of the crops grown by Organate Foods. The appeal of growing more crops locally is also consistent with the aim of reducing the crops that are imported from abroad. This represents the intention to reduce the 'carbon footprint' of Organate Foods.

Risk management in Organate Foods

Organate Foods has completed the riskiness index and this is set out below. Also, the company has adopted the overall approach described in the five parts of this book, including the completion of the eight templates. The steps set out below relate to the implementation of an overall enterprise risk management initiative. Although the risk management initiative in Organate Foods is described by completing the eight templates, the intention of the case study is to demonstrate that the risk management activities in the company are proportionate, aligned with other business activities and dynamic to change.

Template 1: Riskiness index

The riskiness index represents a status check for Organate Foods and provides an overview of the risk exposures in terms of potential impact of risk events on finances, infrastructure, reputation and marketplace. This is the high level analysis of the risk profile of Organate Foods and helps define the context within which the company will set the risk agenda. The riskiness index is a generic set of risk descriptions that represent the key dependencies for any organization which Organate Foods will need to interpret to suit its own particular circumstances.

Completing the riskiness index has provided Organate Foods with an overview of the riskiest areas of the business. The finances of the company appear to be strong, although there is some concern about the availability of investment funds. It is the infrastructure of Organate Foods that gives some concern, including the availability of people skills, competencies and experience, given that crop diversification is now part of the strategy. However, the greatest area of concern is product availability and supplier unreliability and this is related to the need to ensure greater resilience of the company.

Reputation is also of concern, primarily in relation to product quality. The maintenance of organic certification status is fundamentally important to the continued existence of the company. Organate Foods believes that public perception of the 'veggie box' industry is good and that they are comfortable with its corporate ethics and standards of corporate social responsibility. However, it realizes it is operating in a marketplace that gives them some concern, especially in relation to changing consumer preferences. Nevertheless, the main issue in the marketplace is its supply chain and the availability of a variety of quality fruit and vegetables.

Finances component of the riskiness index		
Code	Description	Score
1.1	Lack of availability (or unacceptable cost) of adequate investment funds	3
1.2	Inadequate procedures for allocation of funds to available opportunities	1
1.3	Poor internal financial controls to prevent fraud and control credit risks	1
1.4	Insufficient reserves for existing and historical liabilities (including pensions)	0
	TOTAL for finances component (maximum 20)	**5**
Infrastructure component of the riskiness index		
Code	Description	Score
2.1	Availability or cost of people skills, competencies and experience	4
2.2	Inadequate premises, plant and equipment to support operations	3
2.3	Processes, including IT infrastructure, have insufficient resilience	4
2.4	Product availability inadequate, including supplier unreliability	5
	TOTAL for infrastructure component (maximum 20)	**16**

Reputation component of the riskiness index		
Code	**Description**	**Score**
3.1	Poor public perception of the industry and/or organization brands	2
3.2	Insufficient attention to ethics and corporate social responsibility	1
3.3	High regulator involvement and compliance expectations	5
3.4	Concerns over product quality and/or after sales service	5
	TOTAL for reputation component (maximum 20)	13
Marketplace component of the riskiness index		
Code	**Description**	**Score**
4.1	Insufficient revenue generation or inadequate return on investment	2
4.2	Competitive marketplace and/or rapidly changing product technology	5
4.3	Poor sovereign economic health and/or lack of economic or political stability	3
4.4	Complex supply chain and/or unpredictable raw materials costs	5
	TOTAL for marketplace component (maximum 20)	15

Score	Potential impact	Score	Potential impact
0	No risk	3	Medium risk
1	Little risk	4	High risk
2	Some risk	5	Extreme risk

Template 2: Risk agenda

The risk agenda includes a consideration of why Organate Foods is launching a risk management initiative and the approach that will be taken. The second template records the risk agenda for Organate Foods. The company wants to take a proactive approach to risk management and constantly improve the level to which risks are managed.

Risk agenda for Organate Foods	
Risk management context	Organate Foods realizes it is operating in a risky environment. However, the resources and expertise within the company are adequate to successfully manage most of the risks it faces. Nevertheless, there may be a need to occasionally use specialist industry/risk consultants.
Risk strategy	Organate Foods intends to take a proactive approach to risk management, especially in relation to risk events that could reduce crop availability, variety and quality. Retaining organic certification status is critically important to the company, but is not considered to be at risk.
Risk attitude/appetite	The attitude to risk in Organate Foods is that all investments and incidents that could cost more than £20,000 will be subject to board consideration. The board will determine strategy, tactics, operations and compliance activities based on consideration of the level and nature of the risk, the rewards available, compliance requirements, controllability of the risk and the availability of alternative actions.
Risk resources	The successful management of risk is considered to be within the competency of the existing board. Additionally, Organate Foods will use specialist industry and risk consultants to provide advice on key aspects, such as crop production, food safety, safe working practices and procedures for importation of food.
Risk protocols	Organate Foods has identified the need for risk management protocols in several areas of activity and has produced written protocols for the key risk areas, including: • Risk management activities, such as undertaking risk assessments. • Retaining organic accreditation and ensuring food hygiene. • Internal financial control and accounting procedures. • Employment legislation, including health and safety at work.

Template 3: Risk record

Organate Foods undertook a structured risk assessment of the key dependencies described in the riskiness index to identify the significant risks it faced. In total, five significant risks were identified that could have an impact greater than the £20,000, which was established as the benchmark test of significance. In summary, these significant risks are:

- crop failure and/or crops rotting in storage because of adverse weather conditions;
- loss of key supplier reduces availability, quality and/or range of fruit and vegetables;
- loss of organic status and/or cross-contamination with non-organic products;
- reduction in customer willingness to pay extra for organic fruit and vegetables;
- reduction in demand because of change in customer tastes and/or competitor behaviour.

This list of risks is entirely consistent with the information recorded in the riskiness index. In particular, Organate Foods does not anticipate significant risks associated with its finances. The company has decided that the risks of crop failure and loss of a key supplier need to be managed proactively. The company has also decided that the remaining three risks need to be monitored, but in each case the current level of risk is tolerable.

The purpose of the third template is to record the analysis of each of the five significant risks. For the sake of example, only the first risk related to crop failure is analysed in this case study.

Risk record of potential impact	
Risk reference	Infrastructure Risk Number 1.
Nature of risk	The risk of crop failure because of disease and/or adverse weather conditions and/or crops rotting in storage because of adverse weather and/or storage conditions. This risk is associated with company processes (or infrastructure), but could have a significant impact on the finances, infrastructure, reputation and/or marketplace.
Potential impact	The magnitude of the risk could be in excess of £100,000 and is now considered more likely to occur following the adverse weather conditions in the current year.
Tolerability of event	Failure of crops, exposure to crop diseases and deterioration of crops in storage have been tolerable, until the current year. It is now considered that this risk is no longer tolerable at the current level and controls additional to those set out below are now required. Loss of crops occurred both because of unexpected storm and frost and also because of conventional deterioration during sustained wet weather.
Existing controls	Mitigation currently in place includes careful selection of crops and the growing conditions required, together with the routine inspection of crops as well as prompt response to any deterioration of crops in the fields and in storage.

Template 4: Risk consequences

Template 3 provided an analysis of each significant risk, but it is for the board to decide how they are going to respond to the risk analysis. Completing Template 4 for each of the significant risks will enable Organate Foods to evaluate the potential consequences for strategy, tactics, operations and compliance in each case. The response (Template 5) to each significant risk will then be based on the consequences that are identified for that risk. The record in Template 4 relates to the significant risk of 'crop failure and/or crops rotting in storage because of adverse weather conditions'.

Record of anticipated risk consequences	
Risk reference	Infrastructure Risk Number 1.
Risk consequences	The immediate consequence of crop failure will be the inability to deliver the variety and quality required by customers. This will result in additional costs to use an alternative supplier and/or loss of customers. It is now considered that adverse consequences are more likely to arise and additional actions need to be taken.
Plans for reducing risk	Given the recent adverse experience, Organate Foods has decided to implement tactics to reduce the consequences should the risk materialize. Additional measures will be introduced, as described in Template 5, and the overall intention is to diversify crop production and also seek alternative suppliers.
Monitoring of the risk	Additional crop inspections will be introduced, especially in relation to the extra crops that will be grown. Also, monitoring of weather conditions would be more routinely undertaken, so that early indication of possible crop failures will be obtained.
Governance of the risk	Specialist advice will be sought, especially in relation to crop diversification. Also, investigations will be undertaken into the availability of more weather-resistant varieties. The board will monitor actions as part of the enhanced risk governance that will be introduced.

Template 5: Risk response

Template 5 records, on a control by control basis, the additional actions considered necessary to improve management of the risk. The record that is shown in the template relates to the additional control to be introduced in response to the significant risk of 'crop failure and/or crops rotting in storage because of adverse weather conditions'. Completing this template will enable Organate Foods to document the implementation of the risk action plan. This will require a description of the additional and/or modified control that is required, who is responsible and the deadline for completion. The company will also plan additional actions in respect of the risk 'loss of key supplier reduces availability, quality and/or range of fruit and vegetables'.

In circumstances where the current level of risk was considered to be tolerable, no additional controls will be introduced. Organate Foods has decided that 'the loss of organic status and/or cross-contamination with non-organic product', 'reduction in customer willingness to pay extra for organic fruit and vegetables', and 'reduction in demand because of change in customer tastes and/or competitor behaviour' are all risks that can be tolerated at the current level. This is because the board consider that the risk is so unlikely to occur that they do not need to either improve the controls or make specific plans to be implemented should the risk materialize. If the risk event does occur, it would be treated as a crisis and the board will concentrate all its efforts on resolving that crisis.

Risk control introduction and/or modification	
Risk reference	Infrastructure Risk Number 1
Additional control	Diversification of the crops grown by Organate Foods on its own farmland to reduce the consequences of failure of one of the crops. This control may also be introduced at the same time as investigations are undertaken into the availability of alternative suppliers.
Implementation date	Given the extent of crop failures during the current year because of adverse weather conditions, implementation of this additional control during the next growing season is considered to be essential.
Responsibility for action	The operations manager is responsible for crop selection and production and, accordingly, is responsible for the planning and implementation of the crop diversification additional control.
Monitoring action	Monitoring implementation of the control will be the responsibility of the board and, in particular the responsibility of the non-executive chairman. Monitoring will be undertaken by checking progress against a project plan and by monitoring the development in the fields of the alternative crops being grown.

Template 6: Risk communication

Template 6 will enable Organate Foods to communicate risk information to relevant stakeholders. The template will help record the arrangements in place for the administration of risk management. Roles and responsibilities need to be allocated, together with the committee terms of reference, record keeping requirements and communication arrangements. In the same way that Organate Foods decided on proportionate resources being allocated to risk management, the extent of the risk architecture and the associated written records will need to be proportionate to the risks faced by the company.

Risk communication arrangements	
Roles and responsibilities	Organate Foods has decided to allocate responsibilities according to the range and nature of stakeholders. The general manager will be responsible for communications with the regulators and financiers. The operations manager will be responsible for communications with staff and neighbours. The commercial manager will be responsible for communications with customers and suppliers.
Risk architecture	Organate Foods has decided that there will be no board sub-committees. Accordingly, the individual board members are responsible for designing risk management strategy, implementing necessary controls and monitoring risk performance. This structure will require board members to challenge each other's behaviour if it is to achieve satisfactory standards of risk governance.

Risk communication arrangements	
Record keeping	Recordkeeping requirements will align with the significant risks faced by Organate Foods and the additional statutory requirements that apply. Recordkeeping requirements will include: • Details of crop yields and quality. • Records necessary to maintain organic certification. • Customer sales volume and complaints frequency. • Supplier contracts and contract fulfilment. • Health and safety and other statutory recordkeeping requirements.
Internal communications	Internal communications will extend to training and instructions to staff, as well as including the following reports to the board: • Monitoring of risk actions, indicators and performance. • Update at each meeting on the status of the five significant risks. • Details of the annual risk assessment for Organate Foods. • Ad hoc reports to advise changes to the status of significant risks.
External reporting	Specific stakeholders, such as financiers and regulators, may require detailed reports and/or routine meetings. The board should prepare risk information for these reports and meetings. Additionally, Organate Foods produces a weekly newsletter to advise customers on crop availability. The newsletter is also used to give advice on recipes and invite feedback from customers.

Template 7: Stakeholder expectations

Consideration of stakeholder expectations will enable Organate Foods to ensure it is delivering what is required and is managing the significant risks it faces. In the case of Organate Foods, it is the expectations of customers and suppliers that are most immediately and/or continuously at risk. Accordingly, Organate Foods will consider the expectations of these two groups of stakeholders routinely and confirm that the current level of risk to the fulfilment of stakeholder expectations is appropriate.

Stakeholder expectations	
1. Customers	Expectations of customers include: • Good quality and variety of ethically sourced fruit and vegetables. • Reliable weekly delivery service at a reasonable cost.
2. Staff	Expectations of staff and employees include: • Good working conditions with ethical employer. • Reasonable pay rates with overtime opportunities.
3. Financiers	Expectations of financiers and sponsors include: • Secure credit worthy organization with transparent accounts. • Return on money loaned/invested at the agreed rate.
4. Suppliers	Expectations of suppliers and contractors include: • Agreed terms of trade and prompt payment of invoices. • Fair negotiations when there are contract adjustments/deviations.
5. Regulators	Expectations of regulators include: • Compliance with all applicable rules and regulations. • Cooperative attitude with willingness to share best practice.
6. Society	Expectations of society include: • Trustworthy and ethical company that supports local communities. • Farming techniques that acknowledge rights of neighbours.

Template 8: Risk assurance

Template 8 provides confirmation that the management of Organate Foods is able to give assurance to all stakeholders that significant risks have been identified and analysed. Completion of this template is also an opportunity for Organate Foods to confirm that the improvements achieved will be maintained in future. Following completion of Template 8, Organate Foods will be able to establish a cycle of updating all templates on a routine basis. Review of the completed templates should take place at each board meeting and updating the templates should take place on (at least) an annual basis.

Risk governance arrangements	
Assurance requirements	Assurance on risk management activities will be required by all stakeholders, but especially regulators and financiers. Because there are no board sub-committees, the assurances provided to external stakeholders will be based on the assurances received by the board itself.
Sources of assurance	The sources of assurance available to the board will be based on information provided by the individual directors. The three executive directors have clear responsibilities for activities within the company and dealings with the various stakeholders. Given the nature of the business, assurance in relation to many of the risks can also be obtained by physical inspection of crops and/or records.
Three lines of defence	Organate Foods recognizes the benefits of separating responsibility for: 1) designing risk strategy; 2) implementing controls; and 3) monitoring performance. However, in a small business like Organate Foods, the board has responsibility for these three activities. Therefore, ensuring satisfactory risk governance will rely on: 1) executive management; 2) support and information from advisers, regulators, financiers, customers and other stakeholders; and 3) the chairman of the board. In this way, the company will implement a proportionate version of the recommended three lines of defence model.
Challenging assurance	In order to challenge assurances provided, the board recognizes that individual board members must challenge each other, under the stewardship of the chairman. The ability to challenge successfully will require the chairman to keep up to date with developments in organic farming.
Assurance reports	The types of assurance reports that are required by stakeholders will include the following: • Status of significant risks and implementation of additional controls. • Details of risk events and regulator activity. • Customer and supplier feedback reviews. • Crop yields and other business success measurements.

Further reading

Organic Centre Wales (2008) *A Farmer's Guide to Organic Fruit and Vegetable Production*, www.organiccentrewales.org.uk

APPENDIX 2

Templates – Implementing a risk management initiative

The following templates are available for download from the *Risk Management* book page at **http://www.koganpage.com/strategicsuccess**.

Template 1: Riskiness index

The riskiness index is intended to act as a status check for the organization. It provides an overview of the risk exposures in terms of potential impact of risk events on the organization's finances, infrastructure, reputation and marketplace. Completing the riskiness index will establish the risk profile of the organization and this will provide the starting point for the development of the risk agenda.

Complete the riskiness index and identify the score out of 20 for each of the four components; the higher the score, the greater the exposure of that component to risk. Completing the riskiness index will provide an indication of whether the greatest risk exposures exist to the:

- finances of the organization;
- robustness of the infrastructure;
- reputation of the organization and the sector within which it operates; and/or
- nature of the marketplace in which it operates.

Finances component of the riskiness index		
Code	**Description**	**Score**
1.1	Lack of availability (or unacceptable cost) of adequate investment funds	
1.2	Inadequate procedures for allocation of funds to available opportunities	
1.3	Poor internal financial controls to prevent fraud and control credit risks	
1.4	Insufficient reserves for existing and historical liabilities (including pensions)	
	TOTAL for finances component	
Infrastructure component of the riskiness index		
Code	**Description**	**Score**
2.1	Availability or cost of people skills, competencies and experience	
2.2	Inadequate premises, plant and equipment to support operations	
2.3	Processes, including IT infrastructure, have insufficient resilience	
2.4	Product availability inadequate, including supplier unreliability	
	TOTAL for infrastructure component	

Reputation component of the riskiness index		
Code	Description	Score
3.1	Poor public perception of the industry and/or organization brands	
3.2	Insufficient attention to ethics and corporate social responsibility	
3.3	High regulator involvement and compliance expectations	
3.4	Concerns over product quality and/or after sales service	
	TOTAL for reputation component	
Marketplace component of the riskiness index		
Code	Description	Score
4.1	Insufficient revenue generation or inadequate return on investment	
4.2	Competitive marketplace and/or rapidly changing product technology	
4.3	Poor sovereign economic health and/or lack of economic or political stability	
4.4	Complex supply chain and/or unpredictable raw materials costs	
	TOTAL for marketplace component	

Score	Potential impact	Score	Potential impact
0	No risk	3	Medium risk
1	Little risk	4	High risk
2	Some risk	5	Extreme risk

Template 2: Risk agenda

The risk agenda includes a consideration of why the organization is launching a risk management initiative and the approach that will be taken. The risk agenda will be related to the size, nature and complexity of the organization, as well as the information gained by completing the riskiness index. Together, these form the risk management context. The organization needs to decide whether it will take a passive or pro-active approach to risk management and identify the resources that will be dedicated to risk management.

This template should be completed to record the risk strategy for the organization, together with a description of the overall attitude to risk, including consideration of the risk appetite. Information is also required on the resources that have been allocated, as well as the risk management protocols that will be developed.

Risk agenda for the organization	
Risk management context (see note 1)	
Risk strategy (see note 2)	
Risk attitude/appetite (see note 3)	
Risk resources (see note 4)	
Risk protocols (see note 5)	

Guidance notes

1 The risk management context is defined by the results of completing the riskiness index and the size, nature and complexity of the organization, including consideration of the regulatory framework.

2 The risk strategy for the organization should identify whether risk management is being undertaken for passive or proactive reasons, including details of risk improvement targets, where these have been established.

3 The attitude to risk should define how willing the organization is to take risk and give details of the benchmark tests that are considered significant, including the role of top management in the making of risk-based decisions.

4 The resources that will be allocated to risk management need to be identified including decisions on outsourcing some risk management activities to a specialist contractor, such as security, business continuity and/or health and safety.

5 The range of risk protocols that will be produced needs to be identified, such as the standards and procedures that will be introduced for the management of risk, including details of how risk assessments will be undertaken.

Template 3: Risk record

Completing the riskiness index in Template 1 provided the organization with an overview of its risk profile. Completion of a risk record for each significant risk produce a risk register for the organization. This will provide information on the specific risks that could have a significant impact on the success of that organization. Completion of this template for each significant risk will require the analysis of significant risks to the finances, infrastructure, reputation and marketplace.

This template should be completed on a risk-by-risk basis to record details of the risk events that have been identified that could have a significant impact on the organization. Identification of these risks can be based on a consideration of the objectives of the organization and/or the features that must be present for the organization to be successful. These features are often referred to as key dependencies. In other words, risk identification can start with a review of the objectives and/or the key dependencies for the organization.

Risk record of potential impact	
Risk reference (see note 1)	
Nature of risk (see note 2)	
Potential impact (see note 3)	
Tolerability of event (see note 4)	
Existing controls (see note 5)	

Guidance notes

1 A unique identifier should be assigned to each risk for ease of reference and unambiguous identification; the risk reference assigned can also be used to indicate the nature and/or location of the risk.

2 Description of the risk event and how it might be caused or triggered, including information or data on previous experiences with a related risk event, both within the organization and in relation to similar events that have affected competitors.

3 Analysis of the potential impact on the finances, infrastructure, reputation and/or marketplace, in terms of the likelihood and magnitude of the risk event and the relationship to objectives and key dependencies.

4 Decision on whether the level of risk identified during the analysis is tolerable for the organization, including consideration of the controllability of the risks and the nature of the business imperative associated with the risk.

5 Mitigation currently in place and standard of risk control that is achieved by the existing controls, compared with the level of risk that is required, including consideration of the efficiency and effectiveness of existing controls as well as regulatory requirements.

Template 4: Risk consequences

Completing the risk record in Template 3 on a risk-by-risk basis will provide the organization with an overview of the specific events that could have a significant impact on the organization's finances, infrastructure, reputation and marketplace. Completion of this risk consequences template will enable the organization to decide the management actions it intends to take in response to the significant risk events. Template 4 is designed to enable the organization to evaluate the potential consequences for strategy, tactics, operations and compliance for each of the risk events.

This template should be completed on a risk-by-risk basis to record the results of the risk evaluation for each of the potentially significant risk events. Undertaking the risk evaluation and recording the results in the table will enable the management of the organization to decide what actions need to be taken to make the anticipated consequences of each of the identified risk events tolerable.

Record of anticipated risk consequences
Risk reference (see note 1)	
Risk consequences (see note 2)	
Plans for reducing risk (see note 3)	
Monitoring of the risk (see note 4)	
Governance of the risk (see note 5)	

Guidance notes

1 A unique identifier should be assigned to each risk for ease of reference and unambiguous identification; the risk reference assigned can also be used to indicate the nature and/or location of the risk.

2 Evaluation by top management of the anticipated consequences for strategy, tactics, operations and/or compliance should the event occur, including consideration of the consequences of the risk event for the future of the organization.

3 Recording of plans for reducing level of risk in order to make the risk tolerable in relation to the anticipated consequences should the risk event occur, and the intended rewards of continuing with the activity to which the risk relates.

4 Details of how the level of risk is monitored, including details of measurements taken of risk performance and/or the leading and trailing indicators that would result in a change in the level of risk.

5 Confirmation of specific governance arrangements related to the risk and any statutory or mandatory reporting obligations, including consideration of the risk attitude/appetite of the organization and the ability to improve risk control standards.

Template 5: Risk response

Undertaking the evaluation of the risk consequences for each of the significant risks and recording the results in Template 4 will enable the organization to decide what, if any, further actions are required. Template 5 records, on a control-by-control basis, the additional actions that have been selected; these relate to the introduction and/or modification of controls. Completion of Templates 3, 4 and 5 will enable the organization to analyse risk exposures, evaluate risk consequences and document the actions that should be taken to make each risk tolerable.

Template 5 should be completed to record information on the additional and/or modified control measures that will be introduced. This will enable the organization to document the implementation of the risk action plan. It will require a description of the additional and/or modified controls to be introduced, allocating responsibility for undertaking the further actions and the deadline for completion.

Risk control introduction and/or modification	
Risk reference (see note 1)	
Additional control (see note 2)	
Implementation date (see note 3)	
Responsibility for action (see note 4)	
Monitoring action (see note 5)	

Guidance notes

1   A unique identifier should be assigned to each risk for ease of reference and unambiguous identification; the risk reference assigned can also be used to indicate the nature and/or location of the risk.

2   Detailed description of the nature and type of the additional control that is proposed, ensuring that there is sufficient information about it to make the implementation of that additional control fully auditable.

3   Deadline for completion of implementing the additional control, including information on how details will be communicated to relevant stakeholders and how progress with the implementation will be monitored.

4   Responsibility for implementing the additional control, including details of the resources that will be required to design and implement the control, as well as ensuring that the new control meets all statutory and regulatory requirements.

5   Details of how the successful implementation will be monitored, the actions that will be taken to measure the efficiency and effectiveness of the control, as well details of the arrangements for reversing the new control, as appropriate.

Template 6: Risk communication

At this stage the organization will have completed the riskiness index, identified the risk agenda, undertaken assessment of significant risks and established the need for additional and/or modified controls. Template 6 is designed to enable the organization to communicate all of this information to relevant stakeholders. The extent of risk communication required will depend on the size, nature and complexity of the organization, as well as its risk agenda.

This template should be used to record details of the risk management roles and responsibilities, as well as the risk architecture for the organization. This template will enable the organization to focus on how it will communicate the risk messages that have been developed by completion of the previous templates. The need for risk record keeping, internal communications and external reporting should be recorded.

Risk communication arrangements	
Roles and responsibilities (see note 1)	
Risk architecture (see note 2)	
Record keeping (see note 3)	
Internal communications (see note 4)	
External reporting (see note 5)	

Guidance notes

1   Details of the risk management roles and responsibilities that have been allocated in the organization, including the responsibilities associated with the setting of risk control standards, implementing those standards and monitoring compliance.

2   Details of all the relationships between individuals and/or committees or groups with risk management responsibilities, including reporting and monitoring structures.

3   Information on the recordkeeping requirements within the organization in relation to both the static standards, procedures and protocols and the more dynamic records, such as incident reports, performance reports and the results of risk assessment activities.

4   Information on the internal communication within the organization on risk management matters, including procedures for sharing risk management documents and risk escalation procedures, as well as risk management training, information and instructions.

5   Details of the external risk management reporting requirements, especially those that relate to reporting incidents to regulators and the requirements to provide regulators and other stakeholders with routine updates or status reports, including whistleblowing arrangements.

Template 7: Stakeholder expectations

Having completed the previous templates in order to plan and implement the risk management initiative, the organization will now need to validate the actions that have been taken. Completion of Template 7 will facilitate validation of the approach that is being used and confirm that all significant risks have been considered. Many organizations start with a consideration of stakeholder expectations when planning the risk agenda; this is a perfectly sound approach. The sequence of templates offered here place the consideration of stakeholder expectations as a post-implementation validation for the risk management initiative.

This template provides an opportunity for the organization to identify all stakeholders and their expectations. This exercise will serve as a check to ensure that the organization is delivering what is expected and is managing the significant risks that could undermine the delivery of stakeholder expectations. If the current status of the organization with regard to the delivery of stakeholder expectations is found to be unsatisfactory, further review of Templates 3, 4 and 5 will be required.

Stakeholder expectations	
Customers (see note 1)	
Staff (see note 2)	
Financiers (see note 3)	
Suppliers (see note 4)	
Regulators (see note 5)	
Society (see note 6)	

Guidance notes

1 Identification and delivery of the expectations of customers and clients, including those related to the quality, availability and value for money of the goods and services provided by the organization.

2 Identification and delivery of the expectations of staff and employees, including those related to pay/salary, working conditions and employment prospects offered by the organization.

3 Identification and delivery of the expectations of financiers and sponsors, including those related to financial security, financial procedures and return on investment offered by the organization.

4 Identification and delivery of the expectations of suppliers and contractors, including those related to terms and conditions of trade and fair and ethical treatment by the organization.

5 Identification and delivery of the expectations of the regulatory authorities, including compliance with rules and regulations, willingness to share good practice and a cooperative approach towards regulators.

6 Identification and delivery of the expectations of society, including corporate social responsibility and ethical treatment of all stakeholders by the organization.

Template 8: Risk assurance

Having completed the previous seven templates, the organization will have implemented a comprehensive risk management initiative. This will enable the organization to provide risk assurance to relevant stakeholders on the management of the significant risks faced by the organization. The means by which this risk assurance is provided should be recorded in Template 8. Completion of this template is also an opportunity for the organization to confirm that the improvements achieved will be maintained in the future. The actions recorded in Template 8 represent the risk governance arrangements within the organization.

This template should be used to record details of how risk assurance will be achieved and the actions that will be taken to maintain the progress that has been made. Following completion of Template 8, the organization will be able to establish a cycle of updating all templates on a routine basis. The frequency of updating should be appropriate to the size, nature and complexity of the organization.

Risk governance arrangements	
Assurance requirements (see note 1)	
Sources of assurance (see note 2)	
Three lines of defence (see note 3)	
Challenging assurance (see note 4)	
Assurance reports (see note 5)	

Guidance notes

1   Details of the risk assurance requirements that are required by different stakeholders in the organization, especially regulators and other stakeholders that are vitally important to it.

2   Information on the sources of assurance available within the organization by way of both static documents and dynamic reports, including those giving information on risk performance and leading/following indicators.

3   Details of the three lines of defence structure that exists in the organization to ensure that management is responsible for risk management, appropriate specialist expertise is available and arrangements are in place for independent auditing of performance.

4   Information on risk performance within the organization, including details of how standards are set, how they are implemented and the arrangements for monitoring of performance, so that these can all be challenged by top management.

5   Details of the risk reports that are produced by the organization, and the stakeholders for whom these are intended, to ensure that they are designed in a way that fulfils all statutory reporting requirements.

INDEX

(*italics* indicate a figure in the text)

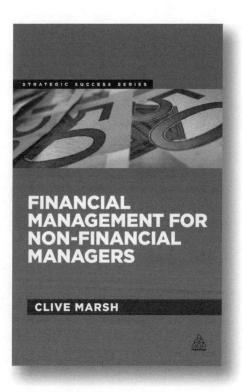